GOLD STARS

GOLD STARS

*My journey from being works-driven
to Presence-motivated.*

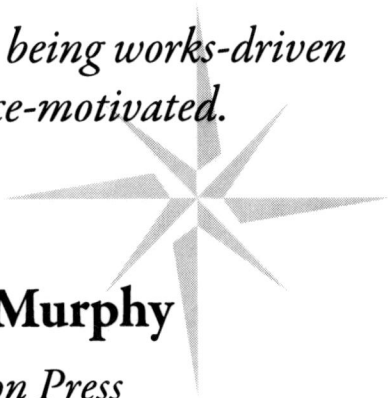

Judy Murphy

Xulon Press

Xulon Press
2301 Lucien Way #415
Maitland, FL 32751
407.339.4217
www.xulonpress.com

Xulon
PRESS

Scripture quotations taken from the New King James Version (NKJV). Copyright © 1982 by Thomas Nelson, Inc. Used by permission. All rights reserved.

Scripture quotations taken from the Holy Bible, THE MESSAGE REMIX The Bible in Contemporary Language. Copyright 2003 by Eugene H. Peterson. Used by permission. All rights reserved.

Edited by Xulon Press.

Printed in the United States of America.

ISBN-13: 9781545610251

Table of Contents

Foreword

For those in the church growing weary of performance based religion, please allow me to introduce a new book called Gold Stars or a better way that we can easily label graced-based relationship. Like Judy Murphy, (author, artist, pastor) so many of us began our Christian walk based on our need to perform, or our need for self-righteousness, our need to merit God's acceptance and if we could just be good enough and follow the rules we earn a star.

Many years ago, being led by Holy Spirit, Judy began in earnest to seek God's face through prayer and scripture and God began giving her revelation on three small words of Jesus, "it is finished". These small words seem to open a door for Judy allowing her to move from the paradigm of Doing into Being.

Doing has the Law for its foundation, while Being is established through the gift of God's grace. Doing quickly becomes works for righteousness powered by performance, while Being is works of righteousness powered by grace. Further, Doing has many bosses driving us, while Being is simply releasing what God has deposited in us as Holy Spirit leads. Doing requires great effort, while Being's only requirement is rest. Doing is how you see you, while Being is how God sees you. Doing is mankind reaching up to God, Being is God reaching to mankind.

As Judy skillfully navigates the reader through the maze of self-performance into this place called grace, readers will identify with every page. They will discover that our concerns over performance began at an early age and are shared by many, spanning in some cases, decades. While Judy's pen reveals the concepts of grace, supported by a vast array of scripture, Holy Spirit will begin to connect and even amplify the differences and freedoms that many now enjoy.

Her learner objectives are clear and precise flavored with great humor. You will laugh and cry as you relive your own list of rules starting even in Sunday school and cry when you realize that God has given you everything you will ever need, want or desire. His grace is defined in 1st Cor. 1:30 (NKJV) where we read that we are in Christ Jesus, who became for us wisdom from God--and righteousness and sanctification and redemption—

Revelation 13:8, part b says and at the least, suggests that God's Lamb was slain from the foundations of the world. Gold Stars agrees with Graham Cooke regarding this scripture when he and others say that God found us and knew us in Jesus, Eph. 1:4; before He lost us in Adam. His love for mankind was established in Jesus from before the foundations of the world even though His love was not manifest in the flesh until Calvary.

When we see the frustration of mankind and the macrocosm of humanity searching for answers, Gold Stars is both timely and life-changing as we remember John's words in John 1:17 declaring that the law, doing, came through Moses while grace and truth, being, came through Jesus.

As Senior Pastors of Florence Vineyard Church, Judy, working with Holy Spirit has mentored my wife, Beverly and me along with our congregation, and week by week we see our congregation being transformed from Doing into being. Our web site post weekly power point teachings along with audio and we average between eight hundred and eleven hundred hits each month from around the world and by faith, the Gold Stars message of His loving grace is being received wherever people have ears to hear.

George Sisemore
Pastor, Florence Vineyard Church
Florence, Ore.

CHAPTER 1
GOLD STARS

As long as I can remember the goal of a believer in Jesus Christ is to go to heaven and on the way, do everything in your power to take as many others as you can with you. While living out my life, my mission is to become more like Jesus, thus showing the world what they are missing and what they need to do to reach the goal. Although goals may differ from one church denomination to another, they almost always include one focus: to please God. This can be done in many ways from weekly penance to a daily rigorous effort of service and commitment, depending on the church of your choice.

Whatever group you found yourself joining, you are welcomed with open arms by those who have traveled the path before you. Well trained in doctrine and dogma, these folks are always eager to take you under their wings and provide you with helpful hints to enhance your success and strengthen you on your way to the goal. It can be a little confusing because these hints vary in so many ways from one group to another that sometimes you need a lesson or two in discerning the difference between good, better, and best. The best, of course, is the door you happened to walk through. In any case, if you follow the directions, you will reach your intended goals and be a happy camper. Right?

If you are honest with yourself right now, your thoughts are ranging from "I wish" to "Mission: Impossible," and you would be right. How do I know? Been there, done that. I spent about thirty years in the performance-driven mindset of a hamster wheel. I believed that God required a certain level of performance worthy of His favor. I needed to make Him happy. I needed to feel worthy of His love. More than anything in the world, I wanted Him to smile at me.

Those years of tightrope-walking sent me right into a crisis of faith. I felt a vague dissatisfaction in my soul, a black hole of despair that seemed to be growing daily, and I hadn't a clue how to overcome it. Something, somewhere, was very wrong. I knew what life was supposed to look like and feel like, but mine looked nothing like the travel brochure. I would sing praises about joy unspeakable and full of glory, while having the distinct feeling as though I was being pulled down into a pit. What was wrong with me?

I was able to keep up a good façade for a while, pretending that everything was just fine. But when I was alone with my honesty, fear began to raise its ugly head. So I kept up the show, trying to make the darkness go away by ignoring it. There comes a day when the darkness threatens to blot out the light. I needed answers now. I was desperate for answers but didn't know the questions I should be asking.

I needed to take serious inventory of my life. Was I devoted to Jesus? Was I whole-heartedly given to Him? Absolutely and unequivocally. Did I love God and desire to live for His glory? Yes, with everything in me. How was my prayer life? This was constantly on my mind, accompanied by fervent prayer, praise, and worship in every position known to man. My desire to serve the Lord was what I was all about.

Therefore, this terrible darkness was a source of indescribable anguish. Something, somewhere, was not right. I felt no joy, had no peace, and did not feel loved—you know the list. To utter my heart's cry was unthinkable. The belief system that defined me would be questioned. It would lay open my entire life to suspicion. The very foundation of my life, of who I was, would come under the heat of scrutiny. I couldn't bring myself to say it.

I knew the Holy Spirit lived in me. That experience was supposed to be the cure-all for any unpleasant feelings I might encounter in life. I was supposed to feel joy—abundant joy. I was supposed to have peace that passed all understanding. And love, the biggest and best of them all, was the hardest loss I felt.

In a word, I was miserable but too proud to admit it. I was desperate and needy but could not bring myself to admit to any need, let alone a spiritual one. (Oh, by the way, did I fail to mention that my husband and I were pastoring at the time?) Not only was I brought up in the faith, but I was trained in it as well. I fully believed that God had called me to ministry. During that era the basic belief was that if you were not pastors, you were not in "the ministry." We loved our lives and those the Lord gave us to love. Therefore, my particular struggle had the potential to undo me on many levels. What is a pastor's wife supposed to do in a situation like this? I felt like the cross-reference for the word *hypocrite* in the dictionary would take the reader to: see Judy Murphy.

Facing my frustrations I had come to the obvious conclusion that I was lacking. Big surprise. I already knew that. Some changes must be made; I knew that, too. Obviously, God doesn't need to change, so I needed to properly diagnose the problem inside of me and make every effort to fix it. And that is exactly what I did.

THE BIG "FIX-IT" LIST

One highlight in all of this was the fact that I was trained to tell people what to do when they came to a crossroad situation in life. I had heard these remedies all my life and had shared them from time to time. These are solutions you must do to get back on track or things you need to do to keep from getting derailed in the first place.

Number one on the list to fix me was, of course, spending more time in God's Word. That's great advice. His Word to me is like air to breathe. So, I upped my focus on Bible reading. I read the Old Testament. I read the New Testament. I devoured Bible studies designed to teach you how to hear from God. I was determined to find my answer. Hours, days, and months of sleepless nights later, I found myself deeper in the muck of discouragement. Without question, the Word of God is life-giving and all-powerful, but for me, during this experience, the words just looked back at me. I hung on to scripture like a drowning man hangs on to a life preserver. My life depended on it. I felt a little glimmer of hope once in a while because I knew what I was reading was true. Even with all that effort, it didn't take long before the darkness settled in again. It seemed like the harder I tried, the more I failed. The promises that spoke of the joy and peace I was supposed to be feeling kept calling to me, but for the life of me I could not access them. They were right before me in black and white, but I had to face the fact that I was not experiencing them.

Discouraged but determined, I continued to the next item on the checklist: prayer. *"That's the ticket!"* I thought. Mixing my Bible studies with more deliberate and purposeful prayer with a good helping of faith is bound to help. I have been hearing much about praying in the correct way. Not being sure what that meant, I set out on an endeavor to find out all I could about different prayers and their effects on the soul.

There are about as many ways to pray as there are religions, and even some variations within denominations. There are wonderful resources by people who have discovered secrets to answered prayers. There are words to say and words not to say. There are lists of hindrances to answered prayer to check off. Have I jumped through every hoop? Are my heart issues and motives right? Must I position myself to be heard, or is it all futile effort? Is there something else I need to do or maybe something I have done wrong? My prayers felt empty. I was very discouraged, but I did not know why. As far as I could tell, I was doing everything right. Perhaps you have heard the statement that sometimes prayer just seems to bounce off the ceiling. That about covers it. Back to square one.

Faith is the key. The *faith factor*. We all need to put that ingredient into practice. I heard a lot about *"exercising those faith muscles."* A great faith movement spread throughout the church from 1970 to 1980. Jesus had much to say about faith. I wondered if that was my answer. Did I have enough faith? If not, how would I know when enough was enough? Was my faith rooted in the right source? Was I speaking the correct words to produce the correct results? There are as many aspects to testing and trying faith, as well as a multitude of methods to try. I think I may have tried most of them. I got the same results every time.

After putting my faith to words, going out on a limb, and proclaiming what I believed to be true, I would discern the zip, zip, zip of an invisible saw followed by the inevitable "crack," and of course, a tumble to the ground. I claimed that I did not hear the saw. I confessed that the limb was as secure as the Rock of Gibraltar. But all the words in the dictionary did not prevent my falls. Now I was not only in the same state as where I began, I was covered with bruises. I had come to the conclusion that my perception of faith was not accurate.

Still in the pit, I researched and read everything I could get my hands on that sounded like a solution. They were all very encouraging; they all included wonderful theories and techniques, which should produce positive results in the life of a believer. But for a reason beyond my understanding none of them made any improvement in my situation.

I felt myself sinking deeper and deeper into darkness. I did not know what to do.

HITTING THE WALL

Everything I believed in came crashing down around me. I could not go on like this another minute. It had been the most frustrating year of my life, and I saw no relief in sight. I almost forgot what it felt like to hear God's voice giving comfort or direction or simply telling me that He loved me. What could I do? Should I walk away from God? Should I threaten to leave Him if things didn't turn around? That doesn't work, by the way. Thankfully, God is not moved by my threats.

The bottom line was that I knew I couldn't leave the Lord. He was all I knew, and besides, I loved Him with everything in me. My problem was, I really didn't believe He loved me.

I had all I could stand. I was terrified, confused, and utterly exhausted. I cried out to God and expressed everything I was experiencing. Was I a huge disappointment to Him? Had I failed in my walk of faith? If so, please tell me how. Had I destroyed my husband's ministry? I knew my motives were pure, so why was I suffering this anguish?

Out spilled all of the heartache, the anger, the disappointments, the confusion, and all of the questions that had been tormenting me for over a year. I needed God now more than ever. I was in a very dark place. I didn't know how I got there, nor did I know the way out.

I reminded God of my gargantuan efforts to do everything I knew to do. I served Him with my entire being. I tried everything to please Him and live only for Him, and in the end all I found was a bigger hole in my soul. If commitment, service, devotion, and effort brought you closer to God, why was He so distant? If diligent prayer, Bible study, church stuff, and so forth is the criteria for making God happy, why did I feel He was turning away? If I was doing my best for Him, why didn't He respond to me?

I had been in a crisis of my faith for what seemed to be an eternity. By now I was so discouraged that I couldn't go on. I had come to an end of my efforts. I had earnestly and tenaciously done everything right—everything. That was the hardest pill to swallow. I could say without hesitation that I did everything that could possibly be done. In desperation, again, I cried out to the Lord. Between sobs, trying to catch my breath, I prayed, *"Lord, all my work isn't working!"*

Strangely enough, in over a year of silence, those words got a response. With great tenderness He replied, *"Will you repeat that, please?"* Not knowing if, in my emotional state, this was God, or my imagination, I decided to go with it. *"Okay, Lord. All my work isn't working! You know how hard I have tried to get Your attention. I have gone above and beyond all that I knew to do."* After a few times repeating the original statement, the truth began to chisel a crack in my wall. A light was beginning to pierce the darkness. I began to see an amazing truth that had eluded me for decades.

I knew immediately what had happened. I had reduced God's great grace, His fathomless love, His relentless kindness, and abundant mercy to a dependence on my performance.

At that moment the Holy Spirit moved into my life in a fresh way. I felt a new sensation—freedom! It has never left. Together we dismantled the faulty foundation of my Christian walk and rebuilt it step-by-step with the truth of who God is and who He says I am. I took my first step into grace.

GOLD STARS

Sunday school; where history comes alive, heroes are made and dreams begin. My favorite part of that hour was the stories of Biblical events, complete with pictures, and characters that came alive on a board covered with flannel. I imagined myself right there with Moses as he led his people across the Red Sea. I saw David bring down a mean, angry giant. I was in the multitude that Jesus and His disciples fed with a child's lunch. My imagination soared. It was wonderful.

On the Sunday school wall was a poster with all the children's names. Following each name were gold stars. You received a gold star if: (1) you were present; (2) you brought your Bible; (3) you brought an offering; (4) you memorized a Bible verse, and the big one; (5) if you brought a visitor to class. Those gold stars determined your success in Sunday school. When you looked at the poster, you knew where you stood in the pack. It also showed the world where you stood with God. It was very important to me that my name was at the top or close to it.

That would prove my devotion to the Lord and that I was serious about serving Him with all my heart.

Although the intent of the poster was to learn to develop Christian disciplines and good life habits, in my life it became a gauge, which showed me and the world around me how I was doing. It was a tool to see how I was measuring up to the expectations I was given. We sang, "Jesus Loves Me," but silently knew there were conditions that went along with it. There wasn't a week that I left church without some goal or another I needed to work on. I felt like the old horse trying to reach the carrot hanging from a pole just beyond its reach. No matter how well I did, it was never enough.

As I grew, the poster was replaced by countless rules designed to make God happy, which was of course, the driving force of my life. Nothing else came close to the desire to please the Lord. So I altered my behavior to make that very thing happen. I worked hard at this mission, determined to be perfect, and to remain ever so humble.

I had come to believe that my efforts to serve the Lord made Him love me more. God's favor was in direct proportion to my performance. The underlying motive for whatever I did was, what does God want from me? What is expected of me? That was rule number one, and it applied to every part of my life, every moment of my days. For example:

How about changing my hair style? See Rule #1 (Don't conform to "the world." You must think about how your appearance honors God.)

Did I want to go to a movie? See Rule #1 (What if Jesus were to return while you were in the theater? You would surely be left behind!)

Am I supposed to wear a dress to a picnic? See Rule #1 (Females always wear dresses or skirts—always. I'm not sure why, but that's the rule.)

Do I dare try makeup or nail polish? See Rule #1 (Don't even go there.)

Two straight weeks of revival meetings? Can I take a night off? See Rule #1 (How strong is your commitment to God? Prove it by being in church every time they open the doors. God rewards faithfulness, you know.)

Can I listen to popular music or, for that matter, any music other than from the hymnal? See Rule #1 (Only if you want to go to hell.)

Those issues, and many more, compiled the essence of being a Christian. Above all, I must make God happy. I still hear that message being preached today; it's the same song, just a different verse. Be careful, be careful, and be careful some more. Eggshell walking becomes an art. It is no wonder I found myself in such a state of frustration.

Working like a maniac, frantically trying to do anything and everything to be worthy of God's love is a sure road to a meltdown. It is impossible to balance that attitude with the rest of life. What I failed to realize is those concepts do not come from God. Those rules and regulations came from man's broken thinking and misunderstanding of who God is.

As hard as it was to swallow, I had to face the fact that I really didn't know who God was.

Food for thought:

Have you ever felt like that old cart-pulling horse, trying to reach the carrot just beyond your reach? Despite all of your effort, you get zero results. No matter how hard to work at it, it is never enough but enough for whom?

Is the performance-based religion really from God's heart?

That sure doesn't sound right to me! (Note to self: take a better look at what God's love is all about.)

CHAPTER 2
LEARNING CURVE

Any mechanic, carpenter, or artist will tell you the correct tools can make all the difference in the finished product. They can make the difference between an easy project and one that seems to pile up difficulties. Then, of course, you need to add the knowledge to know how to use the correct tool for the right reason. I was given many tools to aid in my Christian walk. All of them found in scripture and are accompanied with instructions. When I found myself in a crisis of faith, I realized that although I knew the right scriptures, I did not fully understand their truth. Like cement, my mind was thoroughly mixed up and permanently set.

I was terrified. I had been in the desert for so long, and even though change was fearful, I wasn't about to return to the darkness. Was I afraid? Honestly, yes, I was. This new insight had the potential to change me on many levels. I had questions about the validity of my walk with God. Would I be making a mistake by welcoming these changes? I had laid my entire life on these convictions and trusted that they were absolute truth. I had more than a few questions, which only produced another problem: I was taught to never, under any circumstances, question authority. That thought alone filled my mind with guilt. Besides, I was in the position of authority. I was supposed to know what I was doing.

Did I have questions? Yes, I had countless questions. To my delight, I discovered that God wasn't at all bothered by my questions. As a matter of fact, I think He welcomed them. Even further, I truly believe that He had been waiting, with great anticipation, for me to ask them. I knew I was beginning the adventure of a lifetime. The few words I had spoken on that day opened up a universe of potential discoveries that began with a disturbing revelation. It was a matter of grace versus rewards and peace versus striving.

We live in a performance-based society. It works well in schools and the workplace, but when I tried to bring it into my relationship with God, I ran into problems. I discovered that much of my basic understanding about God was untrue. I had developed a set of lifestyle rules, reinforced by my religious training. Following these rules was supposed to show God how much I loved Him and hopefully cause Him to love me more. If I could not find personal significance from the right source, I would resort to my own way of trying desperately to feel important.

Not only were my rules personal, I had so fine-tuned them that I judged other Christians by them as well. These were never spoken out loud, of course, but comparisons become the name of the game in many religious circles. Perhaps you remember back to school days when tests were graded on a curve. There were the super-smart kids who always landed on top. Then there were those poor souls who could never quite get there, no matter how hard they tried. I always hoped to land somewhere in the top half. I needed to keep my ego intact. That is a good way to induce anxiety.

I have good news for you. God does not grade on a curve. As a matter of fact, He doesn't grade at all. My value, my worth, and my success as a person are not based on my performance. God loves each one of us completely. It doesn't matter what I do or don't do. It is never a matter of the condition of my heart or my effort to live a perfect life for Jesus. How do I know this? Because of the cross. The cross levels the playing field completely.

MY NEW BFF

The Holy Spirit entered in a brand-new way. Like the fresh marine air on a hot summer's day, the Holy Spirit refreshed my weary soul. He moved in thoroughly and completely. Although new territory was intimidating and downright scary at times, I was determined to learn what God wanted to teach me. The thoughts and impressions came like breakers on the Pacific.

I had the phrase, "all my work isn't working," down pretty well. It was like a drop of water to my parched, barren soul. The baby steps that followed felt like a major leap of faith into the unknown. As I suspected, much of what I believed to be true about my relationship with God had been built on a faulty foundation. With great tenderness and mercy, the Holy Spirit began to show me where my detour started and how it led to the mire I found myself sitting in. Never, at any time, did I feel anything but tenderness and relentless kindness from the Lord. I began to look forward to every new insight. I looked forward to our times together. My communication with God became very real, as if sitting with a dear friend.

The first thing on God's agenda was to teach me who He is. I thought I completely understood that one. I checked it off the list a long time ago. Together, we began to dismantle the crumbling foundation of my faith and replace it with the solid truth found in His Word. Scripture that had always been there, but I had never really seen. I had known the words, but the truth seemed to be hidden in plain sight.

How long had I been living upside-down? What if my faith, my lifestyle, and my relationship with God were not based on my commitment to Him? What if proving my love to Jesus by what I did for Him was not in His heart? What if my efforts to walk worthy of His Name actually had no influence on God's love toward me?

GOSPEL TRUTH 101

God speaks your language. When the Holy Spirit began to communicate God's truth to me, it was in a way I completely understood. And it was just plain fun! I love to laugh, usually get the giggles at the most inappropriate moment, and just enjoy the presence of the Lord. There were times when, on my commute to work, the Holy Spirit would download a great truth into my heart, and I would laugh all the way to my place of employment. There were other times when those truths brought tears of joy, simply because I was really getting to know God as He really is. I was experiencing Him in ways I didn't know existed. The understanding that the Creator of all we see would take the time and effort or seek me out and converse with me changed me completely.

Most people understand grace enough to get started. They then proceed on their journey by trying to maintain that relationship under their own steam, using their own methods. Christian disciplines (private devotions, prayer, Bible study, witnessing, church service, etc.) become a means of proving our commitment to God.

And that, my friends, was Christianity in a nutshell.

MY VIEW OF GOD

I soon discovered how an accurate understanding of God is crucial to our lives. I came across a story of an ancient man who lived on a volcanic island. The village shaman, or witch doctor, taught the people that their god lived in the fire mountain and would only be appeased by human sacrifice. Every year a sacred ritual was held to appease their god. One particular year, this man's infant son was the chosen sacrifice. He took the baby from his mother's arms and brought him to the *shaman*. The mother was consumed with grief. She could not be consoled, no matter what the villagers said or did to try to comfort her. In this story she made a comment that ran through my heart like an arrow. *"If he had had a different god, he would have been a different man."*

Think about this for a minute. What I believe about God is projected in absolutely every area of my life. My lifestyle, the choices I make, my relationships, my time, my money, my speech: everything about me is colored by my view of God. It especially changes what I think about myself. I knew the Holy Spirit was teaching me the truth of who God was. With His direction, I began replacing my false judgments and opinions about God as I learned and experienced fresh, new concepts.

What would it take for me to believe that God is completely in love with me? What would it take for me to believe that I bring Him so much joy that He can't contain it; He just has to burst out in song and dance? What would it take for me to be so convinced of His love that fear or doubt can't find a foothold?

I wanted my relationship with God to grow past infancy. I needed to get a firm grasp on the truth of His love for me. The truth of the gospel is not about my love for God; it is about His love for me. What if the gospel is not about my commitment to God, but His commitment to me? I had my part working like clockwork but had never considered God's heart for me. What if, in His opinion, it is the other way around? What if, in God's heart, we can't go much farther into His purposes until we understand His love for us?

I believe that religion has taught people to begin by believing in God's love. However, as they mature, they move away from that place of pure childlike faith to making commitment and service to Him the focal point of the Christian life. I think that is upside-down thinking. The more I understand the depth of God's love for me, the more I understand who I am. When that happens, I am ready to move forward into whatever God has for me to do. Growing up in God means growing in our understanding of His great heart.

Both Moses and David used the term, *"the apple of His eye"* when describing God's love for people. I learned what that meant; it is thrilling! It is an archery term describing the attention that the archer has for His target. It is so intense, so focused, that everything surrounding the target fades away, and all the archer sees is the object at which he is aiming.

You are the apple of God's eye. All He sees is you. You may ask how He is able to center His attention on you while doing the same for every person on earth. Don't ask; just believe. This is God we are talking about. Let me tell you a little secret: He loves to break out of the box we put Him in.

This may be an entirely new way of thinking for you. I might be introducing you to a new way of seeing God. It may take some adjustment. That's okay, too. God has a way of sharing that is designed especially for you. Read just a few of the scriptures that describe His heart for you. First John 3:1 tells me God calls you His child. That's amazing! Isaiah 49:15–16 says that God is like a devoted mother. Can a mother forget her child? Even if that happens, God will never forget you. Isaiah goes on to say that your name is actually inscribed on God's hands.

Now that means commitment!

LOVE STORY

I have a confession to make. I am a hopeless romantic. I've always been that way; I am a modern version of Pollyanna. I'm about as sappy as it gets. I came to understand that I am the object of a love so complete that I can't even begin to grasp its depth. I can't comprehend it. I don't understand it. Trying to get my brain around it is an exercise in futility. Thankfully, understanding is not required. Jesus did not say, *"Figure it out.*" He said "*Believe.*" So many wonderful people want to believe; indeed, they will, after they figure it out.

We live in an educated society. (That can be good, and it can be bad.) Each grade level requires more: more learning, more challenges, and more tests. I make the grade, get promoted to the next level, and find more requirements waiting for me there. Up the ladder I go, discovering that the difficulty raises with each level reached. This is called maturity. I have climbed many ladders, trying to reach a specific goal. When climbing the ones about pleasing God, I had super strength, showed colossal stamina, and amazing dexterity, only to discover when I reached the top, the ladder was leaning against the wrong wall.

God's ways are not my ways. That is very true, you know. As a matter of fact I usually find that His way of thinking usually runs in direct opposition to mine. If you have been in church for long, you most likely have heard about the difference between "baby's milk" and the "meat of the Word." There are a lot of biologically mature people who are still spiritual infants. Pastors and leaders want us to grow up by becoming more like Jesus. Their method is usually by learning God's commandments and putting them into practice. That is what mature Christians do. We tend to believe that maturity requires effort; the deep things of God are for those willing to meet the requirements.

This is true! But what is *deep* in my mind may not be what God means by deep. What if my thinking and reasoning are climbing up the wrong ladder? What if working to meet requirements actually takes me away from the truth of the gospel? What if all my work puts my focus on me and takes it off of the Lover of my soul?

That brings me to another question: what is the gospel truth? First Corinthians 1:22 quotes the Apostle Paul as saying, "The Jews require a sign before they will believe. The Greeks require philosophy, logic, reason and debate, then they will draw conclusions whether or not they will believe."

I have some dear friends who are constantly giving people lists of requirements needed to know God, or be saved, or come to the Lord, or ask Jesus into their hearts. There are many ways of saying *believe.* I recently read a list of criteria someone made to inform people how to become a Christian. This is what they called 'gospel'. Interesting reading:

- You must pray the *'Sinner's Prayer,'* (which varies depending on which camp you join.)
- You must learn spiritual laws.
- You must repent of every sin.
- You must ask Jesus into your heart.
- You must be born again. (Unfortunately this did not come with an explanation.)
- You must obey all commandments.
- You must serve the Lord. (I'm not sure what that means, but I think it has something to do with church attendance.)
- You must go to the altar at every service.
- You must dedicate yourself to God, then do it again and again until you have dedicated every piece of yourself.

Requirements! The Holy Spirit posed a question for me: What do you require of yourself? Of others? So I went on a search in the Bible for a specific answer. I found one, spoken again by the Apostle Paul. He only had one requirement: the cross, and one message: Jesus Christ, crucified. Jesus met unequivocally every requirement necessary, and He did it for me. (1 Corinthians 2:2).

It is the love story of all eternity. It is personal. It is intimate. It is about Jesus and me.

I know now beyond any doubt that the Creator of all I see is totally, completely, utterly, and undeniably in love with me. He thinks about me constantly, countless thoughts full of love, and is full of joy, full of compassion, and full of grace, mercy, and kindness. He has no dark thoughts toward me. Every thought of me brings Him great joy. It has nothing to do with being deserving; it has everything to do with who God is.

I have learned to do a lot of "stuff" in over sixty-two years with Jesus, stuff I needed to do to please God: stuff to learn, stuff to achieve, how to get saved, how to stay saved, how to climb my way into God's heart—the list can go on forever. That is, until one day I learned that all that stuff is not only unnecessary, it is a lie. It is not the truth of the gospel. I became so consumed with the stuff that I completely missed the love story.

The cross trumps all efforts to gain God's approval. It demolishes all self-improvement programs. It totally annihilates absolutely every hindrance to God. I will cover much of that in the remaining chapters.

You are the object of incredible love. Many religions have turned a relationship with God into a bartering system. They have made it all about seeking, but God's love story is about finding. Instead of working like a maniac to meet requirements, instead of trying to build up "spiritual muscles," instead of straining to manufacture enough faith, I rest in what has already been accomplished by Jesus for me. It is a love story, I am the central character.

Do you remember the time in the gospels when Jesus took on the role of a servant and washed the disciple's feet? It was an illustrated sermon to show them His love and how to love one another. Peter, whom we all know and love (and who usually entered the room mouth first) adamantly refused to allow Jesus to wash his feet. That was too demeaning an act for the King of kings. Peter did not understand the Savior who gave, not demanded. I was astonished at Jesus' reply to Peter. "If you do not allow me to wash your feet, you have no part in Me" (John 13:8).

Let Jesus wash your feet. Let Him love you.

I have some questions for you. These are questions Holy Spirit asked me:

- What would it take for you to really believe in My love for you?
- What would it take for you to believe that you are my cherished one?
- What would it take for you to believe that you carry My presence?
- What would it take for you to believe that wherever you are, I am?
- What would it take for you to believe that you are My joy?
- What did you do last week to make God love you less?
- What are you going to do to make Him love you more?

CHAPTER 3
GOD 101

LOVE THE LEARNING

I have learned much since I knew it all. I am reminded of the character, Ebenezer Scrooge, from Charles Dicken's short story, "The Christmas Carol." Scrooge put it perfectly when he came face to face with the truth. *"I don't know anything. I never did know anything. But now I know that I don't know!"*

The Holy Spirit makes learning an adventure. He came to move into my life, teaching me about God and about myself as well. The very first thing on His agenda for me was to lead me out of the wilderness and teach me who God truly is. My years in performance-driven religious duty confused me to the point that I did not know God like I thought I did.

Always gentle and kind, He wooed me into God's truth. So often people are told that learning lessons from God is something to be feared. That is not so. I found them to be so enjoyable that it wasn't long before I eagerly anticipated the lessons. I was amazed at what I had yet to learn.

THE PEARL

Sometimes the biggest truth can be found in the smallest examples. There is one very small story found in Matthew 13:45–46: "The Kingdom of God," Jesus said, "is like a merchant seeking beautiful pearls. When he found the one priceless pearl, he sold everything he had to purchase it." It was a familiar story; one I had read countless times. This time was different. The Holy Spirit began to whisper to me, questioning me about this story.

"Who is God in this story?"

"Well," I answered, "God is the merchant."

"Good! If God is the merchant, who is the pearl?"

The light came on in my mind—a new revelation, one that actually goes against every other explanation I ever heard about this story. As I contemplated on these two small verses, the question kept going through my mind: *Who is the pearl? Dare I voice such a revolutionary thought? That would be me!* The truths tumbled out, as a matter of fact.

First, God sought *me* out. I didn't choose Him; He chose me. How many times have we heard that we must "come to Christ" or that we must "find Him?" It is actually the other way around. He searched for me, and when He found me, He put great value on me. Second, He gave everything to purchase me. How many times have I heard that in order to please God, I must be willing to sacrifice everything? I began to see God in a new way. It began a magnificent transformation in my life. The Holy Spirit started to untangle me from years of a belief system that bound me to my efforts, a belief system that, at its foundation, focused on my works and performance.

MY DEBT

Paybacks are a bummer, at least in man's mind. I wonder if God thinks the same way. The answer is in Matthew 18:21–35, another story with a great lesson. It is about owing and paybacks.

It seems there was a man who owed his king a great debt. It was an *enormous* debt, involving so much money that it would look like our gross national debt today. The king wanted to pass severe judgment on him, but he pleaded and begged, promising to pay back every cent.

This was no ordinary king. This king was full of mercy. He was so unreasonably kind that he forgave the entire debt. That alone is amazing. What is astonishing is the man didn't understand what had just happened to him. He had no sense of what the king did for him. He was just completely freed from a lifetime of hard labor. You would think his heart would be filled with utter gratitude, but all he wanted was payback from someone who owed him a few dollars. Go figure. I was reminded that so often that we, as Christians, can have an attitude that looks a lot like entitlement. However, that is not what the Holy Spirit wanted to show me here.

He asked me to read it again. As I was reading it, He stopped me at verse 26 where the man was pleading for mercy, promising to pay the King back. In reality, I think he owed so much money that he wouldn't live long enough to pay it all back. The Holy Spirit prompted me to read it again and then asked if I realized what my response had been to His mercy toward me. I didn't know but had a feeling He was going to tell me. He explained that I had said yes to Jesus and His great mercy toward me, but then, without realizing it, I decided to spend the rest of my life repaying Him for it. Was that not the least I could do? The Holy Spirit taught me that my debt was so great that God didn't want me to think in those terms. What He wanted me to do was just say yes.

Okay. Then, yes. Now what do you want me to do? As per usual, this went on a couple more times when I heard, *"You aren't getting it, sweetheart! Just say yes. That's all. Nothing else."*

"Oh! Oh! Wow!" I shouted yes! Wow! Yes! *Yes*! He didn't want payback. He simply wanted me to accept His free gift. He provided so much insight that day. I was free. I broke out of my prison of fear that I wasn't doing enough for God, that I was a disappointment to Him, and of what others might think. I found my worth in His love and my value in His eyes. I found a security that replaced all fear. When I receive freely, I can give freely, without strings, expectations, or disappointments. Remarkable.

WORKERS COMP

I had the habit of overlooking parts of scripture that I didn't understand. One was found in Matthew 20. It is the story about a man who owned a field and needed laborers. He went out early in the morning to find workers. Again in the middle of the day, he hired more workers. He continued to bring men in until the last hour of the workday. When they all came to be paid, the owner of the field gave them all the same amount. That disturbed me.

I knew this would be another lesson in discovering an amazing truth, so I read it again. It was *still* disturbing to me, and I told the Lord that I just didn't understand.

"What don't you understand?"

"Well," I answered, "it just isn't fair!" There. It was out. It wasn't fair, and I told Him so. His answer blew me away.

"You are right! It is not fair. That is the point. If my grace were fair, it would depend on your performance and your earning power. I am the author of your redemption. I am the One who paid for it. I am the One who maintains it. It is not about rewards. It is about grace." And then I understood. His love is without conditions. His favor has no price tag. It nearly took my breath away.

I continued to learn who God was. The Holy Spirit and I were dismantling the old foundation of my effort-based faith. The new foundation was based on grace and truth. It had nothing to do with what I did or didn't achieve. It had everything to do with what Jesus did for me. "For the law was given through Moses, but grace and truth came through Jesus Christ" (John 1:16).

THE WOMAN WHO SNUCK UP ON JESUS

Hope for the hopeless. I'm sure you have heard that statement, but it has limited meaning until you are faced with a hopeless situation. The woman in Mark 5:25–34 found herself in that exact predicament. She battled a blood disease for twelve years and spent all she had on medical opinions and remedies. Nothing helped.

She was someone who, in desperation, reached for her last hope. She dealt with this disease for a long time and woke up every morning needing to find strength to face the day. And other days she wished she would not wake up.

Dealing with disease is not only physically exhausting, but it drained her of every emotional reserve as well. She just couldn't handle more days. Her dreams had vanished a long time ago. She couldn't even bring her thoughts around to a future of any kind. All hope was gone.

She heard about Jesus. Was He a prophet or a rabbi? She did not know, but every time His name was mentioned, it was followed by stories of miracles, healings, and hope. Perhaps He was her last chance. The rumors were that Jesus was coming to her town. She had to go if it was the last thing she ever did.

Everywhere Jesus went, there were crowds around Him, pushing and shouting for attention. No one wanted to come too close to her, let alone have a one-on-one conversation with her. She would have to brave the obstacles and get close enough to touch Him. Determined, she pushed through the crowd, keeping low to the ground. With Jesus in sight, she reached out. Just a touch, that's all. Due to the crowds, I don't think she grabbed Jesus' robe or even had the time to place it between her fingers. I believe all she could do was brush across it with her hand.

Immediately she felt power enter her body. Jesus felt the very same power leave Him.

Jesus was touched all day. He was in a rowdy crowd. But her touch was different. It was filled with hope. It represented over a decade of courageous endeavors to overcome. Her touch held years of pain and tears. It was from a broken heart in her broken body. Her touch produced something that others did not. Jesus felt healing leave His body.

I believe Jesus did not see her coming.

The Holy Spirit made it clear. This woman did not organize her thoughts to present herself to Jesus. She did not take the time to develop a game plan to approach Jesus. The woman snuck up on Jesus. He did not have time to evaluate her request and prepare an answer. Healing, mercy, grace, and understanding came out of Jesus even when it was unintentional. She simply reached out with no strings attached. She made no bargains, no deals, nor did she try to be worthy.

She received what was in Jesus. Healing was transferred from His body to hers. It was that simple. What God showed me is, He loves me. It has nothing to do with my worthiness or me. It has everything to do with His nature.

HEART OF THE KING

The Old Testament holds one of the most beautiful accounts of grace exhibited anywhere. King David understood God's great mercy. As a young man, his very best friend, Jonathan, happened to be the son of King Saul. They were friends, but treated each other more like family. One would have given his life for the other without hesitation.

This is remarkable, especially considering the way King Saul felt about David. He was insanely jealous of David to the point of wanting him dead. God's hand was on David as his very existence was a threat to Saul.

One of Saul's attacks of rage ended in a plot to kill David. When Jonathan found out, he immediately warned his dear friend. Both of them, understanding the gravity of the situation, vowed to care for the other's family in case of an untimely death.

Sometime later both Saul and Jonathan died in battle. David was anointed king to replace Saul. The incoming king had the power to eliminate his predecessor's lineage, removing any threat to his rule. Saul's family ran for their lives from the new king.

Jonathan had a six-year-old son named Mephibosheth. A servant scooped him up and ran for the hills; in this case, the wilderness called Lo Debar. In their panic they fell, and Mephibosheth was injured, resulting in a crippling condition for the rest of his life.

Years later, King David recalled memories of Jonathan and their friendship. He remembered his commitment to Jonathan to care for surviving family members in case of death. The king asked a servant concerning any remaining members of Saul's family, so he could show kindness for Jonathan's sake.

There was no anger or vengeance in David's heart. He was a man who understood that God had looked on him with graciousness. His success was because of God's greatness toward him. He wanted to demonstrate the same grace to Jonathan's descendants and fulfill the promise made many years before. I love what David did not ask. He did not ask for a quality person to serve in the palace. He did not ask if Mephibosheth was deserving of his favor. He did not put conditions of any sort on this descendant of Jonathan.

Note the servant's response: "*There is still a son of Jonathan who is crippled in both feet*" (2 Sam. 9:2–3). There it is. The stigma. The word that always follows a name. The name Mephibosheth was always followed by the word *crippled*. He was not like the rest of us. He didn't fit in, especially in the palace. Just like many good folks today, events in Mephibosheth's life had left him with a descriptive handle. Some stigmas stubbornly hang on.

David's response was grace-filled. He simply asked where Mephibosheth was, not "where is this crippled son?" or "how handicapped is he?" David refused preconceived judgments. He just wanted to send for him.

Mephibosheth, on the other hand, completely understood his disability. He lived with it nearly his entire life. He became the label that was placed on him. His entire life was filled with stories of what would happen if David ever caught up with him. I imagine he took the news of the king's invitation with great fear. I think he lived in dread of this moment. He had to face that reality. I wonder what thoughts were running through his mind. Were his fears justified? Was David after his head? He surely couldn't run now; even walking was a challenge.

We get a glimpse of their encounter in 2 Samuel, chapter 9. Mephibosheth's anxiety is so strong you can feel it. He may easily lose his life. There is an aspect of this story that is vital to our understanding of God. Mephibosheth, face planted on the floor, spoke to the king words that had defined him his entire life. *What is your servant, that you should look upon such a dead dog as I?"*

The words he heard from David, however, were words he never expected: "Don't be afraid." How foreign to his mind. As long as he could remember, Mephibosheth lived in a state of fear.

Mephibosheth did not know of David's love for his father, Jonathan. He did not know about David's graciousness and kindness. He did not know what was in David's heart. He misjudged the heart of the king.

I believe David looked down on this poor man and was able to feel his years of pain and fear. He looked past the stigma and past the expectations. He looked into his heart and addressed his need for acceptance, for love without condition, for a purpose in life. Just like God does with me. This was David's response to Mephibosheth; "Do not fear, for I will surely show you kindness for Jonathan you father's sake, and will restore to you all the land of Saul your grandfather; and you shall eat bread at my table continually"

Like Mephibosheth misjudged David, I often squeeze God into a box of my making. He is not at all what I imagine. When God looks at me, he does not see the label I go by or the stigmas that are attached to me. His view of me is full of love, possibility, joy, and purpose. He sees the one designed for a specific place at His table.

LEVI

I found my value and worth in learning how God sees me. When I finally laid my efforts down to find some sort of significance on my own, the Holy Spirit began to show me God's point of view. Even those whom society sees as unworthy can find their true identity as God sees it. Levi was one such person. He was a tax collector. I know what people today feel about this subject, but that is nothing compared to the way tax collectors were despised when Jesus walked the earth and with good reasons, too. Israel was overrun by a nation whose brutal strength was constant. Rome conquered the land and ruled with an iron fist. They moved in and took over, making sure everything was done their way. If that wasn't bad enough, they hired Jews to collect taxes for their emperor. Imagine a family member or a neighbor taking your money to give to the enemy.

Not only did these people collect for Rome, they also collected for themselves. They were scoundrels, the lot of them. The conversation around the town square might be something like this: My neighbor knows for a fact that some tax collector took my sister's money, leaving her destitute, and laughed all the way to the bank. Why, a friend in the next town had the same thing happen to him, and the tax man changed his address to an oasis paradise with the money. These guys took dirty to a new level.

While walking through town one spring day, who do you suppose Jesus approaches? You guessed it: Levi. Of all the names to have, Levi is a priestly name. His parents must have had much higher expectations of him. What a disappointment he must have been to them. He was a failure, any way you look at it—a disgrace to his countrymen and a discredit to his family. He was a man decent folks whisper about behind closed doors, a man shunned by the society he knew. Everyone was careful to keep their distance—everyone except Jesus.

Put yourself in this picture. In a busy street, people are reluctantly and defiantly filing by to give their hard-earned money to a dictator. Emotions are running high: anger, resentment, hatred, and bitterness. At a table sits the target of these feelings, someone who is considered the scum of society. He is collecting money from the very people he should support.

A holy man walks by and stops. He stops at Levi's table. He says only two words—"Follow me." That is all it took. I wonder how long Levi had been starving for a word of acceptance. Perhaps he couldn't remember the last time he heard a kind word directed his way. It didn't take two more words for Levi to make up his mind. The next thing you know this Redeemer is joining Levi and his friends for a party. I'm guessing the talk around town went something like this: "I heard Levi quit his job. Did he get a better offer?" I'd say he did. Let's have a party!

Gathered at Levi's house were people from his social class: more tax collectors, street people, shady businessmen, and business women as well. The rest of the town had a handle for folks such as these: sinners and publicans. And there in the middle of it all was Jesus—the Son of God. He was joining the party without loading them with any conditions or requirements for His presence. He seemed to be pleased as punch to be invited and was enjoying the company. I think Jesus was delighted to mingle with them. As a matter of fact, I believe that is exactly where He would go today if He came to visit my town. He would be found where religious people would never enter.

The people gathered at Levi's house were in awe of this Holy man. They had never seen anyone like Jesus. For many, this may have been the first time in a very long time someone out of their circle really seemed to care for them.

During their party, a mob was gathering on the right side of the tracks. They could feel them coming, the pious, finger-pointing, religious leaders, stirring up a cloud of self-righteous dust behind them. Their very presence makes you feel that your existence is against some rule or another. Brace yourself for the verbal beating.

Here they are: the most learned, respected, honorable men in your world. They are always the teachers, never the learners, of which you are often reminded. Experts in everything God related, they are armed and dangerous, prepared to unload some of their wisdom on your poor, unproductive, unsuccessful, miserable existence. The world should stop and take notice. They are about to speak.

This time it is Jesus who speaks. He intervenes with amazing insight into hearts. "Healthy people do not need a doctor," He said, "sick people do. I do not want to spend time with those who deem themselves better than others. By the way, here is a riddle for you . . . see if you can figure it out. God desires mercy, not sacrifice" (Matthew 9:10–12).

Every mouth is stopped. What can they say? They came to accuse and instead were on the receiving end of God's wisdom

Levi, as it turns out, wrote the first book of the New Testament under his new name, Matthew. He wrote about the new covenant that Jesus brought to men. I think that is significant. Matthew understood the difference between law and grace from firsthand experience. They may look similar in appearance, but in reality they are worlds apart.

Levi was the recipient of two belief systems. From the law-keepers, he received judgment, accusations, criticism, anger, and grief. The grace-giver provided unconditional love, mercy, and hope. He received a new name and a new beginning. His future was now one of fulfillment instead of dread. He was full of promise and destiny.

Jesus did not come to condemn, but to save. We quote John 3:16 a lot, but often leave out the verse following. *"For God did not send His Son into the world to condemn the world, but that the world through Him might be saved"* (John 3:17).

GUILTY AS CHARGED

Suddenly the center of attention, the unnamed woman in John 8 was dragged out of bed early in the morning by powerful men bent on her execution. Her sin was adultery. There was no denying it. She was caught in the act. All she could do was stand there, taken directly from her bed and displayed in front of a crowd of people.

Everyone there knew what happens next. The law demanded swift and certain death—for both parties. Wait a minute. As far as the story goes, she was standing alone. Unless I am mistaken, adultery is a two-person affair. Where was the other party in this drama? Something is terribly wrong with this picture. It smells like a set-up to me. With the sentry of strong, religious men, how could her partner possibly have escaped? I don't think he did. I think he simply walked away, his job well done.

There are several things happening at the same time here, each one demanding attention.

The religious mob in this incident had another motive than to see justice done. They set a trap for Jesus, trying to gain necessary proof to accompany their accusations against Him. The accused woman was only a pawn in their plan. That brings a new thought to my mind: why did they select this scenario to trick Jesus? They could have used any number of rules to break. Why choose this woman? I believe it is because they saw something in Jesus that was unheard of in their culture. He put value on every person, women included.

We know what happened next. This woman, standing guilty before a mob of people content in their self-righteousness, all shouting the law's demands, and asking Jesus just exactly what is He going to do about it? It seems Jesus had selective hearing. He simply ignored their demands, bent to the ground, and began writing in the dirt. What was this? Perhaps Jesus didn't hear them; they kept up their accusations. Jesus kept writing.

When Jesus finished writing in the sand, He stood up, and with one sentence defused the entire situation. "*He who is without sin among you, let him throw the first stone*" (John 8:1–11). Another few words written in the dirt made an amazing impact on those who deemed themselves worthy to judge; one by one, from the oldest to the youngest, they walked away.

No one except those present knows what Jesus wrote in the dirt that day, but when He stood up everyone was gone, except the woman who had been caught in sin. Jesus didn't overlook her sin. He didn't whitewash the guilt. He did not ignore her situation. She was guilty; there were no excuses. He asked her the most amazing question; "Woman, where are those accusers of yours? Has no one condemned you?"

"No one, Lord."

"Neither do I condemn you; go and sin no more."

Jesus put out a challenge that morning...if you have no sin, go ahead and throw your stone. The truth is, there was a sinless man there, who did not condemn, but who showed mercy, kindness and freedom. She deserved condemnation; she received forgiveness. Why? I believe Jesus was showing us the Father's heart. The same heart that beats for you and for me.

SCARS

This is a true story. No names have been changed. It is something that happened to me.

I had an accident when I was six years old. Burned with boiling water, I was scalded down the left side of my neck, shoulders, and chest. This happened long before there were burn centers or knowledge about how to care for burn victims. Giving every effort to try to help, I was lathered with Vaseline, which, we now know is the worst thing you can do.

I don't remember much about that day. I remember the boiling water, my dad trying to ease the burning with cold water, and the ride to the doctor. Back at home, covered with bandages, I remember all I wanted to do is sleep. For fear of going into shock, my parents kept me awake until they felt I was out of danger.

The resulting scars were very visible and dictated my value, what I did, and of course what I wore to hide them. All girls want to be pretty, but I believed that I would never be one of them. It didn't send me into depression or trauma; it was just the way things were. I was damaged merchandise. I would never be like the perfect girls I saw all around me.

I grew up and found, to my surprise, that some people didn't even see my scars. They were good friends, regardless of my appearance. The same thing happened when I went to college and began to meet young men. It was there I met my husband who has never once mentioned my scars. Of course, he knows they are there, but he doesn't see them. He sees me.

About twenty years ago as I was praying, it occurred to me that just once I would love to see Jesus. So I asked permission. I wanted to see my Savior. He answered that prayer. I closed my eyes and saw Him in my imagination (which is God-created, by the way). The thing that left me utterly amazed was there, on His body, were the same scars I saw in the mirror all the time.

I can't adequately describe what that did for me and is still doing to this day, but I felt a new depth of His understanding nature. It is personal, it is intimate, and it speaks to the deep things in life. He not only understands physical pain, He understands about the things that touch us in the depths of our soul. He feels what we feel and cannot express, and He comes alongside us with understanding and comfort.

That day I understood a love so deep that it was impossible to find the words to express. I still can't.

For your consideration:

THE TOUCH

In the example of the woman with the blood disease, many can truly understand her suffering, and more important, her questions.

Have you been there? Circumstances beyond your control have left you feeling utterly fatigued and penniless. Your days are spent existing, not living. From where you stand everything is dark.

Well-meaning people try to encourage you. To be honest, you are thankful for them and for their concern, but you already know the answers. Try as you might, you cannot pull this one out of the pit. This time your answer must come directly from God. You must hear from Him or die.

How many times have you worked hard at preparing yourself to be heard? For some reason, we feel we need to convince the Lord to listen to us. I have often approached God in prayer with an underlying feeling that I have to wrestle an answer out of Him. I picked up the idea somewhere that I had something to do with answered prayer; it was almost like it was up to me to lay some groundwork for God to finish His part. Somehow I felt like I had to make myself worthy of His attention.

Simply put, that woman received precisely what Jesus was filled with: love, compassion, health, and strength—every good thing dwelled in Him.

What do you need today? What is in Jesus?

LEVI

I wonder which side of the fence I would have found myself if I had been there. If Jesus came into my town today, would I recognize Him? If so, how would I know that He was God in the flesh? What characteristics would I discern as being from God? Who would He stop and commune with, and why? Who will He be drawn to? Who would accept Him as God, and who would reject Him?

Which brings me to the next question: how do others see me? Some food for thought is, as Christians in today's society, how will we be known?

Too many times we make it very well known what we are against, what we don't like. To the unbeliever's ears, it is translated, "I don't like you." That is a sad commentary for the believing world. I would like to change it, one person at a time. How? Just like Jesus. Ask the Lord what He sees in the heart of someone. (Hint: it will always be positive and hopeful.) Pour God's love into them.

MEPHIBOSHETH

Labels are descriptive handles that tell a story that you wish would remain a secret, such as: there goes Julie, who left her family for another man. Remember Joe, the alcoholic? This is Melissa, a single mom. Have you heard about John? He is scheduled for parole soon. No matter what we may have accomplished or overcome, some stigmas stubbornly hang onto us.

If you understand regret, you understand what it is like to have your name and your value wrapped around a label. True or false, labels can define our lives, our potential, and even our destiny. If you struggle with any memories that tried to bind you to a certain category, ask God about His description of you.

The only thing that defines your value, your worth, and your identity is what God says about you. If you want some information about that, please keep reading. It is woven throughout this book. If you are not receiving positive input about that very crucial subject, find a church or a group of believers who understand the truth of who God really is and who He says you are.

Here's a hint: look for no shame, no guilt, and no condemnation. If that is not what you find, keep looking. You won't find God's truth there. Look for mercy, love, and grace—lots of grace.

CHAPTER 4

WILD THING

Yes, I'm a baby boomer. Right smack in the middle of it all. Looking back, I can see where my religious upbringing muddied the waters of the world around me. We were completely immersed in church activities, keeping ourselves as righteous as possible, and encouraged to mind our manners, and never, ever, under any circumstance question those in authority. The world around us and everything in it were considered evil influences, and if we should get too close, the temptation to become one of "them" would surely overcome all our good intentions.

"WE" versus "THEM"

Church back then held a definite "we" versus "them" mentality. Never spoken out loud, but always felt was the attitude that "we," the saved ones, were absolutely not in any way, shape, or form similar to "them," (those who did not go to church). We were not to associate with them, play with them, visit with them, dine with them, or do anything that came in close proximity to them. We were allowed, however, to invite them to church because of all people, they needed it most. It was a concept that said to those outside of the church, "You are a mess. You are a sinner and need to be fixed, so you need to come to church so we can fix you." Nice, huh? There are words for that kind of thinking, but putting it delicately, I would say it was self-righteousness. Does that sound ugly? That's because it is ugly.

Because of our rules of conduct, I was never allowed to attend dances, concerts, or movies. And I could never listen to the music from hell (The '60s, just in case you were wondering), not if I wanted to go to heaven, anyway. It wasn't until I was an adult that I ventured out into the world of music we now know as "the oldies." I discovered it was actually a lot of fun, and I wish I would have learned some of it as a teenager. Being young at heart, however, I still enjoy the good old tunes. One of which I have chosen as a special song between the Holy Spirit and me. You may remember it: "Wild Thing." It may not have been written to mean what it means to me, but it is extremely descriptive of my relationship with the third person of the Trinity.

I was in a delightful journey of discovery with the One called the Comforter who brought so much joy to my heart and life that those words fit us perfectly. "Wild Thing" was one of those times when He loves to break out of the box I made for Him. I had put God in a severe, fearsome, terrifying box that didn't fit Him at all.

I sincerely apologize if this is offensive to you. If it makes me any more worthy in your estimation, my favorite piece of music ever written is the "Hallelujah Chorus" from Handel's Messiah (which I have sung on several occasions; mezzo soprano). Every time I listen to it I feel like I am in God's very presence. Come to think of it, I am in His presence, every moment, every day. Having been a music major in college, I am acquainted with many classics and hymns of our forefathers, as well as current praise and worship music. I can see God in nearly all of it.

My relationship with the third member of the Trinity was becoming a moment-by-moment encounter into the realm of spiritual things and natural things. They are separate, but they walk side by side. Religion has feared the natural realm, almost to the point of believing that anything there cannot be from the Lord. That is just plain silly. It is all God-created. As a matter of fact, many times the spiritual will spill into the natural realm. That is a good thing, in case you were wondering. If they don't, we won't be able to live as Jesus lived here on earth. I was learning to listen for that familiar voice on a constant basis. He is as close as my heartbeat. I guess if there were one word to describe what I was feeling, and still feel today, it is joy—indescribable, overflowing, unspeakable joy. The joy known only by the free.

DOING VERSUS BEING

Knowing it all can be a heavy burden to bear. Learning that I didn't know it all was both exciting and discouraging at the same time. Having lived my life in the quest for perfection was quite an all-consuming goal but one that I believed must be tried since pleasing God was of utmost importance to my life.

Pleasing meant serving, doing, and working; things that push you up on the perfect-o-meter of "The Christian Life." Pleasing meant rules that polished my image and kept me up on that pedestal. I know that, according to Luke, chapter ten, Jesus told Martha that she could have made better choices like her sister Mary did, but did He realize those people He invited in might be hungry? Sandwiches don't make themselves, you know. There are just things that have to get done, and if I don't do them—well, you know. Anyone with a servant's heart can relate to this. I live in a world where I see things that need to be done, and no one is making an effort to do them. What is a server to do?

I was all about doing. That included doing the regular stuff of home and family, doing extra stuff with church services, studies, and activities, and doing things well so that I would walk worthy of the Lord. It was all or nothing, and I wasn't about to compromise my commitment to God. I had adopted the mistaken concept that put all emphasis on what I needed to do for the Lord. Once in a while I took time to consider what He did for me, which served to propel me further into my efforts to please Him. This philosophy puts the ball entirely in your court. It is up to you to take hold of God's fullness.

"Doing" proved my heart's intention. It showed God, and it showed others, how high He was on my priority list. It was gold stars on steroids. It was what was expected of me—mostly by me, come to think of it. My life was set on "doing" mode from the time I got up in the morning until I went to bed at night.

During that time I was constantly making comparisons with the standard, which was always just beyond my reach. Working! Stretching! Doing! More, more, more! Sounds like an exercise class. It was an exercise in futility, as it turned out. With all the love imaginable and fresh tender mercies every morning, I was learning that doing was not what God required. It wasn't even close.

My husband, Darrell, and I would discuss this issue. If doing stuff to get God's attention was not the plan, then what was it? What did God want from us? Isn't excellence a good goal? There is a big world out there that needed to know there is a better way. We had learned enough to know that doing more stuff was not the answer. What is God trying to teach us? There was something just beyond our understanding. It was so close, we could feel it but had yet to know what "it" was.

What about *being*? What if God's plan and purpose for me had nothing to do with doing the right stuff? What if one of the first steps in fulfilling my destiny is to learn to simply *be* who God says I am? What is *being*, anyway?

The more I thought about this and listened to the Holy Spirit, the more I realized that my purpose in this life was so much more than trying to impress God by doing stuff. He saw something in me, something that only I could be. He created me with a purpose and was all about teaching me how to be the person He created me to be. He gave me everything necessary to fulfill that purpose. As a matter of fact, He designed me for that very thing.

The next question: what is that purpose? First, it is to let Jesus live His life through me. I wanted to be like Him in every possible way. The more I studied this subject, the more I realized that is exactly what God's plan is for everyone. That is why Jesus sent us the Holy Spirit to live in us.

As Jesus was about to leave the earth, He encouraged His followers to wait in Jerusalem for someone He was going to send to us. The Holy Spirit was coming. He would make our bodies His dwelling place. God was changing His address to where we live! He would teach us all about God the Father and His Son, Jesus Christ. He would change us to be like Jesus, from the inside, out. Second Corinthians 3:17–18 tells me that it is the Holy Spirit who changes me from glory to glory, into the image of Jesus.

> The Lord and the Spirit are one; His Lordship sanctions our freedom. A freedom from rules chiseled in stone to the voice of our redeemed design echoing in our hearts! The days of window-shopping are over! In Him every face is unveiled. In gazing with wonder at the "blueprint likeness of God displayed in human

form," we suddenly realize that we are looking at our-selves! Every feature of His image is mirrored in us! This is the most radical transformation engineered by the Spirit of the Lord; we are led from an inferior mind-set to the revealed endorsement of our authentic identity. You are His glory!

And all those years I spent try to change myself!

I remember one day I was praying a very serious prayer. *"Lord, more than anything else, I want to live for You. That is the driving force in my life."* It sounded like a wonderfully perfect prayer to me, and it kind of made me proud that I thought of it. Then I heard that familiar voice. I knew I was in for a happy revelation. This is what I heard the Holy Spirit answer: "I know your heart; it is completely God's, and that is won-derful. May I tweak that prayer just a little? I think you might enjoy this thought. I don't want you to think in terms of living for Jesus. Instead, let Jesus life His life through you."

Whoa! Suddenly all the doing lists and the burdens that came with them were gone. Being. It's that simple? What about all the things that need to be done? They are very real, and can't be ignored. Jobs and proj-ects will get done, all right; don't worry about that. They will be better than ever because all those things became God's fruit being produced in and through my life. I was becoming who God created me to be.

What is the difference between "doing" and "being"? Rest.

JESUS IS NOT A CRUTCH; HE IS A STRETCHER

I love that statement. I was learning to let Him be the One He desires to be in and through my life. What a difference that made to me. I have always loved the Lord; that was never in question. There was always a question mark, however, when I thought about how He loved me.

The time had come to take a good look at this. I was on the edge of another great revelation; one that would change my life completely and is still growing to this day. I had no doubts about my devotion to God, but I could honestly say that I did not fully believe that He loved me. In my mind His love for me still had ties to my efforts and my ability to keep the law. That may be man's thinking, but it is not God's. I wanted to settle this in my heart and mind forever.

The subject matter, if boiled down to one word, is grace. There are so many descriptive explanations about grace. Many are true, at least in part. There are countless aspects of God's grace. We have barely touched the surface. The first thing I learned about grace is that it is unconditional. It is love freely given, no strings attached and no requirements made.

Being thoroughly entrenched in the law, this one took a while to move from my heart to my brain. Yes, I knew in my heart what was true, but to put it into words that made sense took some experiences; some grace stops along the road.

One of the places we stopped and pondered was the famous Sermon on the Mount, preached by Jesus Himself one afternoon. The Bible states that many people heard about Jesus and went to hear what He had to say. You will find it in Matthew, chapters five through seven. After reading it several times, I was very confused about some things in it. I began to see that the Redeemer, the ultimate grace-giver, the lover of my soul, lived under the law. As a matter of fact, He taught the law—on steroids! Not only did He reinforce what the Mosaic Law taught, He raised the bar even higher and then higher still.

For example, right off the bat, in Matthew 5:3–12, Jesus tells us that we should feel blessed when going through difficulties, even when persecuted for the sake of God. Okay, maybe that is fairly reasonable, but let's keep looking.

In verses 21–26, Jesus approaches the subject of anger in relationships. The bottom line is to fix it as soon as possible, or I might be in danger of judgment myself.

Don't stop there. It gets better. The next statements Jesus made are mind-bending. Basically, as far as the subject of man–woman relationships go, to even look at a member of the opposite sex with anything other than pure motives constitutes adultery. Jesus goes farther to say that it would be better to cut off an offending hand or pluck out an offending eye than to allow any impurity in your mind.

Those are only a few examples Jesus gave that give us insight into God's perfect standard. In one word, it is unattainable by humans.

Okay, Lord, I need some help with this one. There is something I am missing here. In actuality, there were several things I was going to learn from these scriptures.

Jesus came to earth. He was God with skin on. God came near. He came to us. I had that backward. In my mind I was always the one approaching God. I had to seek, knock, and find. I had to prepare myself appropriately to be heard by Him. I had to keep myself as pure as possible, my righteousness intact, to be worthy. I must be deserving of God's attention.

There was a day when the Holy Spirit gave me a most remarkable lesson. It was about needing to be deserving of God's love. It was an unwritten law deep in my mind that I must make myself deserving of His attention. That is done in countless ways that kept my mind focused on my attitudes, behavior, and endless checklists followed by repentance, and finally, after I was sufficiently remorseful, forgiveness. Then I started that process all over again.

God was about to change my thinking about all that burdensome baloney. I remember that I was contemplating another attitude adjustment I felt I needed, and how unworthy I was to even go there again. I don't deserve to be loved. I don't deserve God's favor. I will never be good enough. I heard a familiar voice whisper in my mind, "*That's very true, you know.*" (Sit up and take notice— something good is going to happen!) The Holy Spirit continued with the most amazing statement; "*Sweetheart, you don't deserve another heartbeat.*" It made me smile. Then came the giggles. Then outright holding my sides, uncontrollable laughter. Suddenly it all came together.

You see, I was all about being deserving. It was my life in one thought. With one statement the Lord told me that if it were up to my efforts I wouldn't have a chance. It's true! I surely don't deserve another heartbeat. My heart beats because of the love of my Creator. I am breathing in and out because of His great grace. I am able to love, think, and live my life because God loves me. Simply put, I finally realized that everything, my entire existence, was icing on the cake!

REPENT HERE

When Jesus came to men, what was His basic message? Repent, for the Kingdom of God is at hand.

Now, with my imagination being as it is, I can see setting up a tent just outside of town with a sign reading: "Repent here daily. Twice on Sunday." I'm sure people would be lined up for blocks to get involved in this. The stores would run out of tissue, and waterproof mascara would sell at an all-time high.

I don't think so. To my relief, I discovered that I had mistaken the true meaning of the word *repent*. To me it meant long hours spent at the altar, accompanied by great remorse, sorrow, guilt, shame, condemnation, and trying to remember to ask forgiveness for every sin in your life. I was wrong. The word *repent* in the Greek language (into which the New Testament was translated from Aramaic) is *metanoeo*, meaning, to think differently or to reconsider.

What? To think differently? To reconsider something you believed in? This seemed way too simple and totally foreign to what I had known. I studied some more, and to my delight, that is exactly what it means: to change the way you think about something.

Putting that equation into Jesus' sermon that day on the mountainside, He came into a society where the Mosaic Law was much more than a service you attend once a week. It was woven into their daily lives. They lived the law every moment of every day in multitudes of ways. It was not part of their lives—it was their lives completely. The law was their culture, including holidays, events, even meals, and the ordinary things of life. Enter the Son of God into this culture, saying in essence, I have a new way to think about God. It is called Kingdom life.

Now, I don't know about you, but I can imagine what was going through their minds. Israel was under strong-armed leadership that put strict obedience to the law right in their face on a daily basis. Jesus just raised the bar, making the lifestyle even more difficult. In this very famous sermon, Jesus is quoted as saying, "You have heard. . . . but I say. . . ." lifting God's expectations of them beyond their ability to perform. And that, my friend, is the point.

Jesus was giving God's holy standards for life here on the earth. Let that thought sink in for a moment. Are you kidding me? I have a hard time trying to keep up with the Pharisees now, and You are telling me that I'm supposed to be better at this than they are? That's impossible! Exactly.

MY BASES ARE COVERED

There are some memories that are forever burned in my brain. They are about repenting. I have touched on that subject and found it is not at all what I remembered it to be. It seemed that there was a great progression that built up to the actual encounter with God. When you wanted to pray, there were steps to follow. First you had to "tarry" always at the altar. This step could take minutes or hours, often depending on the extent of repentance. If you did not tarry long enough, it meant that you weren't finished, so spend more time at the altar. If my memory serves me right, much of that time was overworking my seriously damaged brain, trying to think of what to do while tarrying. Straining to think of stuff to think about can be extremely taxing. This step always carried serious shame, a great deal of guilt, with a dose of condemnation mixed in. Of course, there must always be tears. Tears proved your sincerity.

In today's society, people are consumed with business. We are much too busy to tarry. I do recall what a friend told me many years ago. He was a P. K. (pastor's kid), so he was always on display as an example. When he was a teenager, he did as expected; he went to the altar to tarry and repent. His mind was blank, but to get up from the altar without sufficient remorse was unthinkable. The most intelligent person that he was, he had a fool-safe plan. When he could not produce real tears, he would put his sorrowful head down, pull out a couple of nose hairs, and the tears would flow. Everyone was satisfied.

I remember being prayed for by some shouters when I was young. At the advice of my mother, I went down to the altar to get more of God. It was an ambush. Several women surrounded me and began to coach me on how to get through to heaven. I distinctly remember different voices saying, Raise your hands! Stand! Kneel! Let go! Hang on! All were shouting at the same time, begging God to hear my voice. Actually, I think it was too loud in there for anyone to hear anything. Did God hear me? Of course, as I lay quietly in my bed, having conversation deep in my soul.

Why do people think that they need to beg? Is that what our God is all about? Not long ago, I witnessed a young man begging and pleading God to bless him and give him a special anointing. He was kneeling. Within moments he was lying face down, then curled up in a ball, then standing with raised hands, and finally, sitting with his head buried in his hands. He was serious. He had to receive what he came for. His value and worth depended on it. There was such anguish in his voice that came directly from his tormented soul. All he needed to do is rest. God knew his heart and had already given him what he desired. He just needed to open his eyes and see it.

What is wrong with seeking God in these ways? People who adhere to these methods clearly don't have a clue as to who God really is and how much He loves them. Their entire existence depends on their own behavior to get God's attention. They are trying to cover all their bases, hoping that when the game is over, they win.

JUMPING COMPETITION

This is totally fiction; even bordering on the ridiculous (just to warn you), so don't try to fit it into your theology. It may, however help you understand the concept.

Suppose (remember, this is just an illustration) that the only way to get to heaven was to jump to the moon from where you stand. Being one who certainly wants to be included in that group, you do everything humanly possible to accomplish the task. You go to jumping conventions to learn, buy the books, and proudly wear the tee shirt to prove that you attended. You have some secrets of the trade, learning them from the best jumpers around. You attend events to demonstrate techniques. Great honor is given to those who can jump farther and higher. You applaud those with the greatest flair and presence. You go home encouraged and determined to put all these things into practice. But the sad fact is, it is impossible. It cannot be done by any human, past, present, or future.

In a very real way, Jesus was saying the same things to those people that day. It is humanly impossible to accomplish God's standard for living. You need a Savior. Jesus was setting these people up to understand their need for a Redeemer to do it all for them.

My next question may be the one going through your mind right now. What about the law? Wasn't it was God's idea in the first place? That is very true. The law was God's plan to keep people in right standing with Him on a temporary installment basis. There were rituals and sacrifices to be made to cover their sin year by year. The law was never intended to make you holy. It was intended to show you God's holiness, and by so doing sin becomes obvious. The law reveals sin; it cannot remove it.

SPEED SIGN

There are some rural parts of the country where there are no speed signs. Travel speed is left to your discretion. Suppose the county decided to put a speed limit on that road. The next time someone was driving it, they had a new rule to adjust to. Now drivers have knowledge of what breaking the law on that road is. When there was no speed sign, there was no rule to break.

Okay, I'm beginning to get it. The law was given to keep God's people in line until our Redeemer came. The book of Hebrews explains it well. Basically the writer (most scholars believe it to be the Apostle Paul) is writing to the Jewish believers about the difference between the Mosaic Law and the God in person, Jesus Christ. They were believers who tried to have a foot in both worlds. Surely they can believe in Jesus' atoning work and adhere to the Law at the same time. It sounds reasonable, if it weren't for the fact that it doesn't work. But why? Why not try to cover all my bases? It seems to me that God would be more impressed by someone who could do it all.

It sounds wonderful, but the truth is that the law can never make men holy. It kept us in line and taught us well, but it will never fulfill God's standard for righteousness. There is a simple reason for this. The law depends entirely on man's efforts. End of discussion.

I have great news, however! Jesus completely fulfilled the law's requirements for you, therefore making God's righteousness available to you without conditions of any kind. Taking the responsibility to fulfill the law's commands completely off of man's shoulders, Jesus carried it all. You will find that throughout Paul's writings, but written specifically here:

His body nailed to the cross, hung there as the document of mankind's guilt; in dying our death He deleted the detailed hand-written record of Adam's fall. Every stain that sin left on our conscience was fully blotted out. His brilliant victory made a public spectacle of every rule and authority empowered by the fall of Adam. The voice of the cross will never be silenced! (Colossians 2:14–15)

Jesus did not die for me, He died as me. He was humankind's substitute to pay the price that redeemed us from sin and sin's effects. God wasn't angry at Jesus or at men. He was angry at the thing that separated us from His love; He was angry at sin. The cross destroyed the very thing that kept us apart. Most people understand that they are forgiven because of what Jesus did on their behalf. That is very true, but only a small part of the truth.

HERE COMES THE JUDGE

Do you want to know what and why you believe? Read the New Testament book of Romans. In it, Paul gives us a wonderful theological thesis for our faith. He explains step-by-step God's way from our sin into His righteousness. It is not by any effort of ours. As a matter of fact, when we try to work our way into righteousness, it actually puts us outside of grace.

To begin with, right off the bat in the first two chapters, Paul first describes those who live a lifestyle steeped in sin and don't care who knows. Then he goes on to describe those who try to live a decent life, obeying God's law, and are good and moral people. It can be compared to a courtroom scene.

Come with me in your imagination. You are there. God is the judge, and mankind is on trial to see if they are worthy of heaven. The blatant sinners don't really care; they even dare you to do something about it. The good, moral, law-abiding people are standing there, shaking their heads at them. Surely their punishment will be swift and just. In a surprise move, Paul states that no one, good or bad, is worthy. Chapter 3, verses 19–20, stops all discussion about the subject. Everyone has given their input; all the arguments for their case have been delivered. Now we wait for the verdict from God Himself. There will be no more discussion.

Remember, it is God's holy standard Paul is talking about here. Men can bring every reason, every good deed and motive to the table. Everything is laid open for all to see: every service provided, every sacrifice made, every prayer prayed, every cent offered, all of it. Men can justify their actions and heart motives with a myriad of excuses. When all is said and done, all mankind stands before the God of the universe whose holiness is beyond compare, the One whose justice is perfect and right every second of every day, the One who is pure light; there is not a hint of darkness or dark motives anywhere around Him. When men begin to compare their gargantuan efforts, even the best ones, with His righteous judgment, there is only one conclusion we can make. Mankind is guilty—every last human without exception.

Everyone in the courtroom comes to that terrible reality. There is absolutely nothing we can do to change the verdict because it is right. It is true. It is just. Every mouth is stopped as this truth hits our brains. Now what do we do?

The next two words take your breath away—*But now!* God had a plan, one that answers every question that could be brought to Him and every solution man could try to find. God is holy; there is nothing He can do that would diminish His holiness. He is just; His justice must be perfect because of His holiness. His judgments are righteous. Always. The only conclusion that can be made is that man is guilty. The judgment must indeed match the sin.

But now, God's righteousness apart from the law is revealed. Someone will pay, all right. It is required because of God's holy and just nature. In a move so brilliant in its perfection, from a heart whose every beat calls for redemption, God sentences Himself.

Jesus, God's very own Son, takes on humanity and all of our sin. Jesus became mankind's substitute to fulfill our sentence. Romans six tells us that Jesus died once (one time) for all (every human). What does that mean? It means that every human in the history of human beings—past, present and future—every human's sin has been judged by God already, in the person of Jesus Christ. It means that every human in history—past, present and future—every human's sin has been punished on the cross, in the person of Jesus Christ. Every human, ever and forever. Jesus took on all sin, all judgment, and the punishment that every person deserved, one time, for all.

The next time you go to work or school or to the grocery store, wherever you are, look around you. Unless you are a recluse, you will encounter people. Every person you see, without exception, their sin has already been judged and punished. It is finished. By God. I had no say in the matter. You were not consulted about this decision. This covenant was between Father and Son.

When the magnitude of that understanding reached my head, I began to realize the kind of love God has for this race called humanity. It changed the way I see myself. It changed the way I see others. We are all the same. God's love levels all hierarchies men will try to make. Pecking order becomes nonexistent. It is all-encompassing and far-reaching. Jesus' atoning work included absolutely every human. This is such a life-changing truth that it needs to be addressed thoroughly, so bravely read on.

Take a few moments to ponder this reality.

What a new thought to my overworked brain! It was so completely different. The reality of it was not what I was used to. The repercussions were endless. My mind was reeling with possibilities. This is the truth of the gospel. It is good news. I took some baby steps into fresh air, and as I did, the Holy Spirit was right there with encouragement, patience, and unbelievable joy.

I'm not sure why, but I had always anticipated some sort of problem or dilemma just around the corner. It seemed impossible for me to not only learn about the good news of the gospel of Christ, but to actually live it and breathe it—work it out, as the Apostle Paul states. I was to the point, however, that I could certainly see the difference between living under the law and living in grace. It is the difference between freedom and bondage.

TEENY-TINY FLY

The Holy Spirit gave me a great illustration during my commute to work one day. It seems there was a smallish fly that found its way into my car. It decided that the best place to be was directly in front of the steering wheel, which means it was buzzing around in tiny circles directly in front of my eyes. My commute was forty-five minutes on a four to six lane freeway and a very busy street in a very big city. The last thing I needed was to be distracted by a fly insisting on buzzing in my face. I tried everything to direct it another way. I wanted his freedom more than he did, but no matter what I did, he was very opinionated about this ride to work. I even opened a window for him, coaxing him to the passenger side. Then I opened the driver's window and tried that. I could tell he wanted out in the worse way, but he was determined, stubborn, and downright obstinate about flying precisely where I needed him not to be. I often wonder how many people "waved back" at me that day. During the day, I thought about that little fly. No matter what I tried, he could not bring himself to accept anything new. Hmmmmm. I think You're getting through, Lord.

Okay, let's look at a couple things.

If you are in a tug-of-war between doing and being; one that places your success as a Christian and your devotion to God entirely on what you do for Him, think about some new thoughts.

When you are consumed with proving your commitment to God by your service to him, the problem becomes, how far along are you? How do you measure your progress? This line of thinking can only measure success by one thing: what you do for God (and how much you do it).

What if God's plan from the beginning has been totally about what He wants to do for us, not the other way around?

How will you have to change your belief system to live in the freedom that God offers?

Remember, repentance is a matter of changing the way you think about something, without drama, stress, or remorse. The Kingdom of God is here.

It may take a little while, or perhaps not, but in any case, make a decision to abandon yourself to God's grace. Put down all information that tells you that you are unworthy, guilty, and full of shame and condemnation. Pick up everything you can that teaches you the truth about the gospel. Hint: it will be filled with God's abundance toward you. It will be all about Jesus' atoning work on your behalf. It will be all about God.

Jesus is not a crutch; He's a stretcher!

CHAPTER 5
LETTING GO

Bungee jumping. Watching those courageous (?) individuals take a flying leap off a precipice—on purpose—makes my knees go weak. That is akin to the feeling I had about letting go of what I lived for decades: how to make God pleased with me.

I knew I could never go back into the bondage of working for favor, having learned so much in a short time about the freedom Christ purchased for me. At the same time, I discovered how deeply entrenched I was in what was familiar—a comfort zone, an unhappy one, but at least something I understood. I was led by the Holy Spirit into something very unfamiliar. I needed more rock-solid truth before I would be ready to jump in. Okay, Wild Thing, lead on!

I imagine He was more excited than I was at that point. He was always available. My ability to receive from God was directly related to my perception of Him. I was beginning to see Him in truth. My heart was melting to His touch. I was changing. A new concept was emerging.

In my experience, that process took some time. Some things came unexpectedly; others took time to think through. I had to rearrange my thinking to match what God was doing in my heart. The Holy Spirit had changed my heart. My thinking was being renewed to believe what I was experiencing was truth. It wasn't enough for me to simply accept the truth without understanding the words that defined it.

I had some understanding about the difference between works and faith. I came to realize that God's love did not depend on my performance. I needed more than that. I needed to know enough to be able to describe the difference. Many people often catch a glimpse of truth, but it doesn't become reality in their life. I needed more than *knowing* the truth; I needed to live it. That added another dimension to my learning process. Living the truth in practice changes the learning process from believing to encountering God.

So many people today are searching for the one thing that will utterly satisfy their soul. I remember catching glimpses of *"something"* new and fresh. It stirred in my soul. It began to take form in my mind. I was eager to know the difference between religious dogma and the truth in God's Word. Much of what I knew was truth; however, just as much of it was not. I needed to know what the difference was and why they were different.

FAITH VERSUS WORKS

In Genesis, chapter twelve, God spoke to Abram. He promised to bless Abram and make him great. God promised to make Abram a great nation and bless him richly. He promised to make his name great and that he would be a blessing to the entire earth.

God told him to move all his family, his belongings, his servants, his livestock, everything—to a place unknown. Abram had a choice to make. He could stay where things were very good, familiar, successful, and secure.

I am pretty sure Sarah asked, "Where are we going?"

And surely Abram replied, "I don't know."

All he had to go on was God's promise to guide him and bless him. The Apostle Paul makes reference to this in Romans, chapter four, when he said, *"Abraham believed God, and it was accounted to him for righteousness."*

Abraham and Sarah were given an amazing promise. They were to be blessed with a child, which was remarkable since they were both over ninety years old. Plus, as an added surprise, the child was going to be their first. What made Abraham so special that God would bless him beyond all expectations? He simply believed God would do what He promised. It was a case of faith versus works.

They waited for the promised heir. Then they waited more. After a reasonable amount of time, (in their opinion), Sarah decided they had waited long enough. Sarah sent her husband Abraham into her maid's tent with one objective: to create a child. It worked. Abraham and Hagar were blessed with a son whom they named Ishmael.

Eventually Sarah did conceive, and Isaac was born, the child promised by God. The child born of the free woman, not the servant. Ishmael was conceived through man's work; Isaac was the one promised by God. Isaac's very existence was based on God's words to Abraham. Ishmael's birth was based on man's ability, schemes, and expertise.

This was one of the first comparisons the Holy Spirit brought to me. I needed to see and prove through Scripture the truth of grace. He brought me back to the Old Testament to show me that His actions toward men had always been from a heart of love and grace.

God did not bless Abraham because he obeyed the commandment. That would have been impossible. The commandments were not given until centuries later through another man chosen by God, named Moses.

COVENANT OF LAW

We all know about the Mosaic Law given to Moses. It was comprised of Ten Commandments plus a couple thousands of others added by religious leaders. It was a covenant between God and man. Each one had a part to play in the covenant. When the terms of the covenant were met, God was satisfied, and the people thrived.

God never acts on a whim. Everything He does is intentional. Everything has a purpose, and every purpose is good. I knew that God always had a purpose, but I supposed most of His purposes had to do with my discipline. I lived in fear of what would come next. I understood the fear. I needed to allow myself to trust. Moses helped me learn trust.

The events of Moses' life were filled with intrigue, adventure, impossible rescues, miraculous dealings with God, and lots of stuff to do. It is one of those times in the Bible where you clearly see the intentionality of God. Every detail of Moses' life had a purpose and fit into God's perfect plan.

He lived on the edge, always wondering what adventure was coming next. One miracle after another released the Israelites from captivity. Miracles would become their daily routine on their journey to the land God promised them through Abraham.

These were not small, ordinary consequences that occurred once in a while. They were huge, mind-staggering provisions that could only be described as miraculous. Each day took a large measure of trust to fight back negatives that were everywhere they looked. At the end of each day, absolutely every need had been met by God's hand. There was not one thing they could do except trust in the Lord.

Moses and his several million family members received God's rules for living a successful life, but we don't often see the moments proceeding that historic occasion. It had been three months since their release from bondage. The Children of Israel were camped under Mount Sinai.

Moses went up to speak to God in Exodus 19:3–6:

> Moses went up to God, and the LORD called to him from the mountain, saying, "Thus you shall say to the house of Jacob, and tell the children of Israel: 'You have seen what I did to the Egyptians, and how I bore you on eagles' wings and brought you to Myself. Now therefore, if you will indeed obey My voice and keep My covenant, then you shall be a special treasure to Me above all people; for all the earth is Mine. And you shall be to Me a kingdom or priests and a holy nation.' These are the words which you shall speak to the children of Israel.

For some reason I had never noticed those words before. They are words of love and relationship. They are caring words, passionate words with great depth of meaning for those who received them. They are words that describe how they were valued and treasured. They are words filled with purpose, devotion, and commitment. They are covenant words; they would never be broken. God did everything for them, and it was in His heart to continue providing, delivering, and supplying every need for those through whom the Redeemer would someday come.

Those words were spoken before God cut a covenant with Moses, giving them laws to live by. It occurred to me, that at the time these words were spoken, the only covenant in place was the one made with Abraham centuries before. I believe He wanted to continue the love relationship with Israel that He had just described, a relationship where people would trust completely on Him and learn to understand His heart for them, where life would be an extension of their connection with their Creator.

What a wonderful offer. He had just given them His heart. Their response was disappointing. Basically, they said, "Thanks so much, God, but we can handle this. We will do it. You can count on us."

If you read further, it was at that point that God appeared fearsome and powerful. It was after their response that Moses was given commandments to live by. It was as if God said, "Okay, have it your way. You want all the responsibility, I will give it to you." Did God still have the same love He showed them during their travels? I believe His heart for them never changed, but He would not force them to love Him. Basically, people usually choose to do it all themselves than to trust God fulfill their needs. From that time until the New Covenant established by Jesus, people lived with the responsibility to fulfill the law themselves. We will take a good look at the New Covenant in a later chapter.

Trust is a big issue for some people; I was one of those. All I saw were the commandments. I did not see the God who would fulfill the covenant Himself.

BEHAVIOR PATROL

"I don't care how high you fly, you'd better walk straight when you land." I hate to admit it, but I can't count the number of times I made that statement. It was my theme song. And I had lots of scripture to back me up. The law extended through the Old Testament, through the New Testament, and right up to the present and into my mind. If you are one who heard me utter those words, I sincerely apologize for putting you in such a position.

I could easily zoom in on the commandments and entirely miss the grace that was shouting at me in the same scriptures. I needed to settle this issue once and for all. I finally saw the difference between works and faith, but the commandments took a little more investigating. I fully believed that living a life worthy of Jesus was a vital part of being a Christian. I still do, but today the emphasis is on who is living it.

How does one walk worthy of Jesus? That's a pretty tall order. You can find it in several places in the writings of Paul. I will use three different translations to gain a good feeling for what Paul is saying in Colossians 1:10–11:

> That you may walk worthy of the Lord, fully pleasing Him, being fruitful in every good work and increasing in the knowledge of God; strengthened with all might according to His glorious power, for all patience and longsuffering with joy. (NKJV)

> Go on a walkabout tour to explore the extent of the land that is yours under His Lordship. Now you can conduct yourselves appropriately towards Him, pleasing Him in every harvest of good works that you bear, meanwhile, you continue to increase in your intimate acquaintance with that which God knows to be true about you. This results in the most attractive and fulfilled life possible. (Mirror Bible Translation)

> We pray that you'll live well for the Master making Him proud of you as you work hard in His orchard. As you learn more and more how God works, you will learn how to do your work. We pray that you'll have the strength of gritting your teeth but the glory-strength God gives. (The Message)

Ephesians 4:1 states:

> I, therefore, the prisoner of God, beseech you to walk worthy of the calling with which you were called. (NKJV)

> The fact that I am in prison does not in the least diminish my awareness that I am in Christ. My complete existence is defined and confined in Him. The detail of your day-to-day life flows from the consciousness of your true identity and worth as defined in Him. (Mirror Bible Translation)

In light of all this, here is what I want you to do. While I'm locked up here, a prisoner for the Master, I want you to get out there and walk—better yet, run!—on the road God called you to travel. (The Message Translation)

1 Thessalonians 2:12:
> ... that you would walk worthy of God who calls you into His own Kingdom and glory. (NKJV)

> ... inspiring you to live in the daily awareness of your true value and identity. In God's opinion you are royalty. (MIRROR)

With each of you we were like a father with his beloved child, holding hour hand, whispering encouragement, showing you step-by-step how to live well before God, who called us into his own kingdom into this delightful life. (MESSAGE)

There are many more examples of commandments given us about how we live and walk on this earth. People don't read their Bibles, but they sure do read their Christians. I placed all of my trust for being a good Christian entirely on my good works. If there were a "Behavior Patrol" chapter in the Bible, I could have written it. Being deserving, walking worthy, and all those wonderful attributes described my goal and my lifestyle. I looked good on the outside, but inside I felt hollow. I needed to know why, and I think I was beginning to see what part of my problem was. The Holy Spirit began challenging my thinking with two words—what if?

What if there was another way to see things?
What if being worthy is not up to me?
What if life isn't a constant struggle with the "old nature"?
What if my value has nothing at all to do with my behavior?
What if I had misunderstood some fundamental truths essential for success as a believer?

It is always so interesting when the Holy Spirit shines a new light on a subject. He began to show me how to see God's Word from His point of view. I was reading in Galatians one day (a fabulous letter written by Paul to correct some thinking). I always believed Galatians 5:16 to mean my performance proves my spirituality. The NKJV states: "I say then, Walk in the Spirit, and you shall not fulfill the lust of the flesh." I had it backwards. Paul is saying, *Let the Holy Spirit lead you and influence you; even take control. That act alone will defeat all cravings of your flesh* (My paraphrasing).

I saw it! All my disciplines, the service, the commitment—all of the behavior modification tactics were not earning power. They were good and noble, even very honorable. But they can never be the foundation of my relationship with God. They are, instead, joyful responses to His love. They are grace in action, the fruit of God's presence in me.

I desired to know about grace to the point that it consumed me. Something bothered me, something kept me from diving in. So many people have unhealthy concepts of grace. I had seen too many wonderful people shout "liberty" in connection with grace, and then show a lifestyle that simply did not look like Jesus. That bothered me greatly. I did not want to go that direction.

What if I had not understood grace? What if I simply needed to know what grace really meant? Grace is not "warm fuzzies" designed to make me feel happy.

Grace is not freedom to sin or a sense of entitlement that you are in a place far and above the need to take care about what you do.

Neither is it an attitude of laziness that says I just don't feel like making any kind of impression. What you see is what you get. I have no intention of changing. Jesus loves me just the way I am, so don't put me under any bondage. No, those descriptions of grace were not for me.

No longer afraid to approach the Lord with my questions, I asked Him about those things. I was delighted to hear that people who believed that way did not understand grace at all.

So, what is grace? The first definition I heard was that grace is God's unmerited favor. Wonderful! That is true, but it is just the beginning. It is so much more—perhaps more than I will ever know. It is the power of the Holy Spirit's presence in your life. It is God's empowering presence that gives you what you need to walk worthy of the Lord. It is strength. It is might. It is what fuels you day by day. In a very real way, it is grace that teaches and trains us and then empowers us to be who God says we are.

WHAT ARE WINESKINS?

You cannot put new wine into old wineskins. It won't work. Why not? What are wineskins, anyway? A wineskin was a goatskin sewn together at the edges to form a waterproof bag. New wine, expanding as it ages, stretches the wineskin. If new wine was put into an old skin, the expanding wine would tear the skin and ruin it all. This illustration was given by Jesus to religious leaders who were interrogating Him about not adhering to strict rules of conduct. Jesus basically said that the New Covenant, which He came to make, would not fit into the Old Covenant of regulations and laws. You have to have new wineskins, fellas.

This covenant was new to the core. The conditions of the covenant were new. The covenant makers were different. The fulfillment of the covenant were poles apart. It simply would not fit into what they knew and practiced. Bringing it home to my heart, it would not fit into my broken theology, either.

Grace and the law do not mix. It is impossible to try to combine them or balance them in any way. This I knew in my mind. I was about to know it completely, from tip to toe. I was getting close; I could sense it. Anticipation was growing in my soul. A door to comprehending the magnitude of God's grace was opening for me. I began to see it everywhere in the Word. How I could have missed this is beyond me. It was as if my understanding were under lock and key, held there by a religious spirit.

THE VEIL

When I read about the crucifixion of Jesus, I also read about what happened inside the Temple the moment Jesus died. A very heavy veil separated the Holy Place, where priests performed ceremonies, from the Holy of Holies. This was for the people's protection. The Holy of Holies was a room that held the Ark of the Covenant and the Mercy Seat. That is where God's presence dwelt. Only one human was allowed to enter the Holy of Holies, and then only once a year when they celebrated the Day of Atonement. On that day, the High Priest was allowed to enter to offer atoning sacrifices for the people. He himself was included in that offering.

Everything must be perfect; no allowances were made for mistakes. From the perfection of the sacrifice and the way it was prepared to be presented to God to the perfection of the High Priest himself, every detail in the process needed to be pure. It was literally a life-and-death situation. If the offering or the priest making the offering were not perfect, they literally had to drag his dead carcass out of the Holy of Holies by a rope that was tied to his ankles, just in case of emergency. People waiting on the other side of the veil would know if things are well, or if they did not go well by the sound of the little bells sewn around the hem of the priest's garment. When they heard the bells, they knew he was still alive. No bells meant there was a job opening for a new high priest.

The veil separated people from God; a situation that had grieved Him from the beginning. At the moment of Jesus' death, the Bible says that the veil (which was approximately fifty feet high and two feet thick) was torn. Who can tear a woven veil that is two feet thick? To add to the drama, the veil was torn from top to bottom. Well, that narrows the choices down considerably. God Himself removed the separation, and the reason for it.

It is important to understand what caused the separation between God and man in the first place. We will cover it in depth shortly, but for now we need to know that the culprit was sin. When sin entered the garden and enticed Adam and Eve to make choices independent of God's direction, they were forced to leave their garden home. That meant leaving the relationship they had with the Lord. It meant that man was now on his own. The precious walks and the communication God and man enjoyed had been severed. Sin separated men from God. That is what needed to be removed from mankind to reconcile us back to God. Sin is what caused the veil to be placed in the Temple.

The cross totally annihilated sin and sin's consequences. When God's own Son carried our sin to the cross, He eliminated the very thing that separated men from God. When sin was gone, so was the veil. In much the same way, the veil that kept me from knowing God intimately was being torn, revealing many layers of truth.

"Blessed be the God and Father of our Lord Jesus Christ, who has blessed us with every spiritual blessing in the heavenly places in Christ"

(Ephesians 1:3; NKJV). Did you know that God cannot bless you any more than He already has?

- What if the issue isn't searching and begging God for a blessing, but it is a matter of asking Him to pull back the veil, revealing what He has already blessed us with in Christ?
- What if the longings of our heart are not answered by working for it or jumping through enough hoops until God decides to give us our key?
- What if Jesus Himself is in passionate pursuit of me, and He has already done everything to bring me to His heart?
- What if all it takes for me to know the truth is to believe it?
- What if God doesn't want to meet me halfway?
- What if Jesus came all the way to where I was, did everything for my response, and is the originator, initiator, and maintainer of my faith?
- What if, in regard to my faith, Jesus really is the author, the one who finishes, and does everything in between?

LAW VERSUS GRACE

Can't I take a little of each, Lord? Does it have to be either/or? What if I tried to balance the two? How am I supposed to just let go of everything I've learned for decades? I wasn't sure I could do that. Although I was struggling a bit, at least I was no longer afraid to ask questions. Believe me, I asked hundreds of them. I wanted to understand grace. I *needed* to understand grace.

I will tell you first what grace is not. It is not a license to sin. We are covered with enough grace to last several lifetimes. Some people think that gives us the freedom to make unwise choices without consequences. Rasputin was one of those people. He believed that since grace shows God's goodness, then the more I sin, the more God is glorified. I think we just passed ridiculous and went straight to idiocy. If that is your opinion, I'm afraid you don't understand grace at all.

There are those who have a sense of entitlement; they think they can live a life that does not produce Godly fruit because they believe that His grace has covered it all. I am sorry to say that these folks do not understand grace, either. It is obvious that they do not reckon the old sin nature to be dead. Dead men don't sin. For those kind of people I say, to be sure, there are natural consequences for your actions. They are exhibiting a false representation of who God really is.

I have heard it called cheap grace. In other words, we must have some sort of requirement, something I need to do to achieve salvation and justify the grace given to me. I have to pay something. People who adopt that reasoning join those that don't understand grace. Grace is extreme in its cost. It just doesn't cost you.

The transition from law to grace isn't easy, especially for Pharisees like me. We are used to having the entire responsibility for our spiritual walk rest squarely on our own shoulders. Jesus came to take that responsibility off of our shoulders and onto His. That was God's plan from the beginning. To try to secure any part of our redemption by our own effort is a slap in the face of Jesus Christ. It invalidates the cross and strokes our ego.

Is it difficult to believe that God so loved the world that He gave His only Son? Do we have trouble believing Jesus did not come to earth to condemn us but to heal us? Those things are not a problem. The problem lies in the fact that God did it all without any help from me. Any attempt to add to or adjust Jesus' complete work on the cross is going backward into the law. First Corinthians 1:30 states that Jesus became for us our wisdom, righteousness, sanctification, and redemption. I don't see anywhere that my efforts (however grand they may be), are included in the process.

THANK YOU, PAUL!

One of the most used arguments regarding law versus grace is found in Romans, chapter seven. You know the one. Paul was very accurately describing the frustration we face when we take charge over our own lives. This chapter explains what living under the law looks like. It is not describing life under the freedom of the cross.

Basically, Paul explains life ruled by rules. I will quote from the Mirror Bible a few verses that will clear up the confusion about this subject. Look in Romans 7. Paul sets the subject matter with the first verse: "I write to you in the context of your acquaintance with the law;

you would agree with me that laws are only relevant in this life. A wife is bound by law to her husband while he lives; any further legal claim he has on her ends with his death." That makes sense. Okay, keep going. "The very same finality in principle is applicable to you, my brothers, in the (crucified) body of Christ you died to the system of the law; your inclusion in his resurrection brought about a new union. Out of this marriage (faith) now bears children unto God (righteousness).

Very understandable so far, and even enlightening! Before we go too far, we need to understand that the problem we have is not with the law, but with sin. Verses six and seven explain:

> But now we are fully released from any further association with a life directed by the rule of the law, we are dead to that which once held us captive, free to be slaves to the newness of spirit-spontaneity rather than age old religious rituals, imitating the mere face value of the written code. The law in itself is not sinful; I am not suggesting that at all. Yet in pointing sin out, the law was in a sense a catalyst for sinful actions to manifest. Had the law not said, "Thou shalt not covet," I would not have had a problem with lust.

The law revealed sin by showing God's perfect standard. Once I recognized that fact, I began to try with every ounce of strength in us to live by the commands of the law. That is a wonderful goal; that is very admirable but absolutely impossible. Let's continue with verse fifteen:

> This is how the sell-out to sin affects my life: I find myself doing things my conscience does not allow. My dilemma is that even though I sincerely desire to do that which is good, I don't, and the things I despise, I do. It is obvious that my conscience sides with the law. Willpower has failed me; this is how embarrassing it is, the most diligent decision that I make to do good, disappoints; the very evil I try to avoid, is what I do.

The law can never make me holy. Simply because it depends on me to fulfill it. Before long the frustration brought me to a breaking point. There must be an answer. It is again found in Romans chapter 7: "*The situation is absolutely desperate for humankind; is there anyone who can deliver me from this death trap?*"

Thank you, Paul, for your transparency and honesty. The inner turmoil is real. The questions are valid.

How could a loving God give rules to get His approval that are totally impossible to attain? That is near cruelty. But that is what is taught by people who are supposed to understand spiritual things. People are shown a God whose demands are beyond human ability and then are told that the consequences of sin is a death sentence. The result: lives become an endless cycle of endeavor, failure, repentance (who knows when it is enough?), forgiveness (again), and then the process starts all over again. Is there any end to this way of life? Is there any relief from the guilt and shame experienced every time people don't make the grade?

This was much more profound than I realized. It can go deep into personal worth; the system by which people find their value. It is futile to strive for an unknown conclusion. Not only did this affect me personally, but it found its way into relationships, which only compounded the issue. I soon found myself buried in layers of confusion, fear, and doubt. I needed answers when I didn't even know what the questions were.

Paul gives us the answer by first giving us the name of the problem. Sin. The solution to sin? It is not the law; we already discovered that. The truth is that God became our solution!

Romans 7:24–28 (Mirror Translation) says:

> Thank God! This is exactly what He has done through Jesus Christ our Leader; He has come to our rescue! I am finally freed from this conflict between the law of my mind and the law of sin in my body. Now the decisive conclusion is this: in Christ, every bit of condemning evidence against us is cancelled. The law of the Spirit is the liberating force in the life of Christ . . . Spirit has superseded the sin enslaved senses as the principle law of our lives.

The beginning of chapter seven is concluded by the fact that the only way to be free from the law is by death. Jesus Christ Himself provided that freedom for us when He took upon Himself the sin of the world. When He died, humanity's sin died with Him. In resurrection He forever sealed the issue of sin in our lives by providing us with the exact same Spirit that raised Him from the dead. Mankind is under a new law—the law of the Spirit of life in Christ Jesus. It trumps everything else. The Mosaic Law served God's great purpose by keeping men in touch with God until Jesus came to fulfill the total requirements that were in it. That law was temporary. Redemption is eternal.

Romans seven has been misunderstood, misplaced, and used as a tool to pound people into shape. The gospel of Jesus Christ is good news. Those who cannot accept that fact need to take themselves out of the equation, believe that God wants to do it all, and let the cross have its way in their lives.

We are now dead to the law, dead to sin, and alive to God by the Holy Spirit who takes up residence in us. To that I say, *Yea God*!

JOHN, THE DISCIPLE JESUS LOVED

Jesus loved John. John actually laid his head on Jesus' chest; his love for Jesus was real enough to show emotion. I can imagine listening to that heartbeat, filled with love so extreme that it cost Him everything. John's love for Jesus went past the words, the declarations, and the ways the others showed their devotion to Jesus. There was something different about John. It did make me question, however, why John was the only one described in such a way. It is almost as if Jesus loved John more than the others. I knew there had to be a reason, so I did some investigating. My discovery was delightfully inspiring.

There are two scriptures that have those particular words. One is found in John 21:20. After Jesus' resurrection, He appeared to hundreds of people, including, of course, the men who followed Him during His ministry. John was one of them. He wrote the gospel of John, the fourth book in the New Testament. The statement about being the disciple that Jesus loved was made during breakfast at the seashore, when Jesus called the fishermen to shore to eat and fellowship. It was a simple statement describing the conversation on the beach. Peter was asking about John, there described as the disciple whom Jesus loved. That is how John is described by others.

The remarkable thing about this statement is that there is only one other scripture that says the same thing; it is also in the book of John. So, these words are used two times in the gospels, both in the book of John. No one else made that statement. None of the other disciples used those words to describe John. Why do you suppose that is? I believe it is simply because of all the disciples, John got it. He understood the love of Jesus. I am quite sure that many people felt and believed in Jesus' love but not to the extent that John did.

During the last agonizing days of Jesus' life all the disciples ran away. All except for one: John. It was a time of heartbreaking distress, confusion, and fear. Even though Jesus warned them of what was ahead of them, this was far from their minds. This could not be happening—not to Jesus, not to their Messiah. Their torment drove them from the scene. It was too unbearable.

One man did not run. The man who understood God's love refused to leave Jesus' side. He went through the terror with the strength that only great love can give. Before He died, Jesus gave John the honor of taking care of His mother after He was gone. There was trust there that can be given only to one who loves deeply.

Being loved is the most powerful force in the world. Knowing that I was loved without condition was the last thread holding me to the oppression that had me in its grip for decades.

COME ON IN; THE WATER'S FINE!

Yeah, right! I've heard those words before. The temperature is a sizzling ninety-five degrees outside, and I'm sure I can see tiny icicles forming around the pool edge. I admire people who just take the plunge. I am not one of them. I inch myself into the water. If it were possible to move slower, I would. I would have to be desperate to just jump in.

Desperation pretty much describes how I wanted to abandon myself to God's grace. What was stopping me? Not a thing I knew of. I decided to believe. I believed that He loved me without condition. I believed that I was the apple of His eye. I believed that His grace was not earned but given without requirements. I let go of all the effort, all the work, and the reasoning that they made a difference with God.

I wanted to know Him. That's all. I finally let go of everything else and let Him love me the way He wants to. There is a word for that: freedom: Freedom from religious tyranny. Freedom to let go of fear and worry that I will fail. Freedom to believe what God says about me is true, when I feel like it and when I don't. Freedom from the bondage that had kept me from experiencing everything God longed for me to have.

Lord, give me the courage to surrender, and the freedom to fly.

The children of Israel had no choice but to depend completely on God for absolutely every human need. Wow. What an amazing thought. I can relate, at least partially, to that dilemma. It is being out of options, at the end of myself. The children of Israel found that is actually the best place to be. I want to be there by choice.

I think I will go back and read through all the "what ifs" in this chapter. What if it is all true?

CHAPTER 6

YOU ARE NOW ENTERING THE GRACE ZONE

Requirements are everywhere I look. Glancing around, even inside of my home there are multitudes of requirements necessary to maneuver correctly in this life. My cupboards are full of them; they are on every box, can, or bottle in the kitchen. Those brave souls who just want to watch a show, a game, or a movie on their television are inundated with requirements. Venture outside, and I see them everywhere—on billboards, road signs, and advertisements. Unfortunately the church has adopted some requirements as well.

Accompanying every requirement I faced was always another hoop to jump through, proving my worth and, measuring my commitment to the Lord. I was just plain tired of them all. I had heard about them as long as I could remember. The problem was that after all my efforts to do everything well, on the other side of the hoop were dozens more to practice on. Religious requirements, and my ability to fulfill them, measured my value and worth as a human being, and most of all, as a believer in Christ.

Although I would never question the requirements, they often puzzled me. Some made no sense, while others seemed to be in word only and not followed through to daily life. How could someone praise and glow in church and then complain all the way home? Why were our lives scrutinized when no one really cared about our hearts? And the biggest question was, why am I not allowed to question these practices? I was about to learn something remarkable that would answer these questions forever. In truth, God is the only one qualified to make requirements because He is the only one able to fulfill them. And that is exactly what He did. The righteous requirements of the Law were fulfilled by Jesus Christ when He gave His life for mankind. End of discussion. There is no argument that stands against the success of the cross. The only thing left to do is agree with it. As strange as it sounds, that is the most difficult thing for many people to do.

SHOULDER ANGELS

I am surely admitting my age, but I remember the old television cartoons where a character has a decision to make. Poof! A lovely little white angel appears on one shoulder giving righteous instructions. Poof! A little devil appears on the other shoulder telling the subject to listen to him instead. I had believed as long as I could remember that I still had a sin nature to deal with. There was always the other voice in my head urging me to listen; it was my old, sinful nature. Yes, Jesus saved my soul, or spirit, and I was going to heaven someday, but I would always fight my sin as long as I had breath in me. Therefore, fulfilling righteous requirements kept sin at bay and made God happy with me. I was about to learn that all of that was not only unnecessary, it was a lie. It is not the gospel of Jesus Christ.

Shocking? You bet it is! Paul states that the only thing he wants to preach is Jesus Christ, crucified. All of it—all the works, all the effort, all the fretting and worrying about being good enough, all the times I went to the altar to get saved over again, absolutely everything that put my work in the equation is worthless. It amounted to nothing. Actually, it is described as garbage.

What if your struggle for righteousness is over?

What if God has no intention to "fix" anyone?

What if He is not interested in a "cleaned-up sinner'?

What if He doesn't have a list to check off, determining your value and worth?

What if the Christian life is not about the endless struggle to do better?

What if religion has misunderstood some vital things about God?

I would like to share some truths that have completely set me free and how the Lord walked with me through the process. Are you ready for the adventure of a lifetime?

IT IS FINISHED

I am an artist. I love having something creative to do. I love the process that takes you from idea to reality. The finished project always fills me with joy. One day I asked the Holy Spirit what Jesus meant when He said, "*It is finished!*" What was finished? What was accomplished, and how was it achieved? His answer absolutely revolutionized my life. "What if your starting point as a believer was the finished product? What if you began the race at the finish line? What if the race was already won before you began?"

I needed to think this one through. I had always believed that the Christian life was something acquired one success at a time. The goal (being like Jesus) was way out there somewhere in the far-distant future. Seeing myself in the present, and looking at what I believed the finished product was supposed to look like were not similar in any sense of the word. There were so many things I needed to get rid of. I had so many requirements yet to accomplish. Burned in my memory was the message that, although I was saved, I was still a sinner with a sin nature that needed to be crucified on a daily basis. When I discovered something that I needed to take away, I would work on it, chipping away at what was wrong with me. There were plenty of areas that needed improvement. I was taught that it would be a lifelong process, so I guess I should get used to it. Religion calls this process sanctification. In essence, it means that I will be forever fighting off the old sin nature to make myself worthy of God's love. By doing that correctly, I will find a way to crucify the flesh.

WOOD STATUES AND SHOPPING SPREES

I remember hearing an illustration about the process of becoming sanctified. There was a man who was carving an Indian out of wood. Someone asked him how he did this. Was there a specific method he used? Were there special tools needed? His answer was simple. "I just chip away everything that does not look like an Indian."

We were in awe of this illustration. We used it on everyone we knew. But the truth is, it a totally false concept. I was all about self-improvement. I believed it was up to me to manufacture what is required to become sanctified.

Another illustration that I heard was about shopping carts. What if there was a spiritual store that had absolutely everything you would ever need in life? You would take your shopping cart down the aisles and fill it to the brim. You had a wonderful collection of strength for hard times, boldness to preach the gospel, the right scriptures for the right situations, the ability to do whatever was required of you—everything you could possibly need was in your shopping cart. You were thrilled, that is, until you came to the checkout counter. Unfortunately, you would have to pay for all those things. Payment must be made.

I discovered that both of these illustrations, as wonderful as they sounded, and with perfect motives, were simply not true. What is wrong with these illustrations? They do not include the complete success of the cross.

THE TOTAL SUCCESS OF THE CROSS

A new thought pierced my mind: what if sanctification is not my responsibility? To say this was a new concept to me is to ask if the Pope is a Catholic. It was a total 180-degree turn-around to what I was taught and believed as truth. What if the war for my sanctification was fought and successfully won by Jesus at Calvary? What if sanctification is a consequence, not a process? The truth is, the word *sanctify* means to set apart for a specific purpose. Sanctified means to set apart.

I am holy already by virtue of being in Christ. I am not sanctified by degrees. If a process requiring my involvement and work was the answer, it would produce more questions than anything else. How would I know when I have "arrived"? It would include another factor to the atonement: the factor of time. Perhaps one day I will be completely sanctified. Really? When, exactly will that be? Hebrews 10:14 says, *"For by one offering He has perfected forever those who are being sanctified (or coming to the understanding of the cross)."* I have heard people say that they will be complete when they die and go to heaven. What does that mean? Death makes me holy? I don't think so, unless you are referring to Jesus' death on your behalf. And that, my friends, is the point.

It is finished. As my representative, Jesus Himself met every requirement necessary to cleanse me, make me righteous, complete, holy, and sanctified. How did He do all that? By removing my sin nature and replacing it with His nature. 1 Corinthians 1:30 states: "But of Him you are in Christ Jesus, who became for us wisdom from God—and righteousness and sanctification and redemption—that, as it is written, 'He who glories, let him glory in the Lord.'"

Most Christians believe that they came to Christ by grace, through faith. They are redeemed, bought by Jesus' blood. After that God sees them through the filter of the cross—through His Son, Jesus Christ. So far, so good; but here is where many people alter the truth of the gospel.

The general belief is that the next step is when the Holy Spirit joins me to aid in life. He came to help me be good and do my best for God. A common phrase is, 'I am a sinner, saved by grace.' If the filter is removed, I am still a sinner. As a matter of fact, many churchgoers firmly believe that they still have a sin nature. This is accepted as truth. It is not the truth. There are many wonderful, believing people who are trying their best to overcome what they consider to be their sin nature, when it was literally crucified with Jesus on the cross. It is dead. Dead men don't deal with sin.

Let's consider this line of thinking. What is the flaw in that reasoning? It leaves out the fact that we have been changed. The general consensus is that men's sin has been covered, but not removed. That is no small difference.

The truth is, my sin was not covered, it was removed from me completely. When John the Baptist saw Jesus coming, he proclaimed, *"Behold! The Lamb of God who takes away the sin of the world"* (*John 1:29*)! Pretty straight-forward, isn't it?

> For it pleased the Father that in Him all the fullness should dwell, and by Him to reconcile all things to Himself, by Him, whether things on earth or things in heaven, having made peace through the blood of His cross. And you, who once were alienated in your mind by wicked works, yet now He has reconciled in the body of His flesh through death, to present you holy, and blameless, and above reproach in His sight. (Colossians 1:19–21)

> For in Him dwells all the fullness of the Godhead bodily; and you are complete in Him, who is the head of all principality and power. (Colossians 2:9–10)

> And you, He has made alive together with Him, having forgiven all your trespasses, having wiped out the handwriting of requirements that was against us, which was contrary to us. And He has taken it out of the way, having nailed it to the cross. (Colossians 2:13–14)

The gospel is good news! Jesus is not an addition to my struggling life, put there to help me make it to heaven. He is not an addition, He is a replacement! Being a Christian is not a matter of getting something. It is a matter of being someone brand new. Being a Christian means that I am someone who did not exist before. It means I am a new creation; a new species of humanity, never seen on the earth before.

> Therefore, if anyone is in Christ he is a new creation; old things have passed away, behold all things have become new. Now all things are of God, who has reconciled us to Himself through Jesus Christ, and has given us the ministry of reconciliation, that is, that God was in Christ reconciling the world to Himself, not imputing their trespasses to them, and has committed to us the word of reconciliation. Now then, we are ambassadors for Christ, as though God were pleading through us: we implore you on Christ's behalf, be reconciled to God.

> For He made Him who knew no sin to be sin for us that
> we might become the righteousness of God in Christ.
> (2 Corinthians 5:17—21; NKJV)

Paul did not say in Christ I *have* the righteousness of God. He says that in Christ, I *am* the righteousness of God. Being a Christian is much more than going to church or even believing in God. It is a matter of identity: God's very righteousness is my identity. It is who I am. First Corinthians 1:30 (MIRROR BIBLE) says, "Of God's doing are we in Christ. He is both the genesis and genius of our wisdom; a wisdom that reveals how righteous, sanctified, and redeemed we already are."

Paul makes an amazing statement in Galatians 2:20–21:

> I am crucified with Christ; it is no longer I who live, but
> Christ lives in me; and the life which I now live in the
> flesh I live by faith of the Son of God, who loved me
> and gave Himself for me. I do not set aside the grace of
> God; for if righteousness comes through the law, (my
> good behavior), then Christ died in vain.

Jesus cured the sin condition in one righteous act. The cross was enough to regenerate all of mankind. Our enemy was completely defeated. He has no more substance. The only power he has over me is when I believe his lies. He is deceitful and cunning and would like nothing better than to cause a Christian to be consumed with angst over their sin nature. Some people use more energy fighting a dead enemy than learning to live in the righteousness God Himself has placed within them.

When Jesus declared, "It is finished!" He was pronouncing the complete fulfillment of the Old Covenant by initiating an entirely new Covenant, one in which man had no part to play. Did you realize that you do not have anything to do with your redemption? Did you know that God did not make a covenant with mankind when Jesus came to remove sin's curse?

The covenant God made with Moses was between God and man. Man fulfilled his part, and God supplied the needs. I had been so trained in the Old Covenant concept of fulfilling my part that I assumed the New Covenant works the same way. Unlike the covenant God made with Moses, the New Covenant requires nothing from men.

This covenant was made between Father and Son. God the Father and Jesus His Son, as well as the Holy Spirit together arranged this covenant. They did absolutely everything necessary to fulfill it. Any attempt by men to add to the work of the cross is gross arrogance and a great dishonor to our Savior. Where, then, does man fit in this picture? We are the recipient of everything that was accomplished. God did all the work; we reap all the benefits. If the cross was enough for God the Father, please say it is enough for you.

FROM VISITATION TO HABITATION

Jesus did not die for me, He died as me. As my substitute, He met every requirement necessary to purify me completely. The Holy Spirit was about to unveil to me the total, utter, and complete success of the cross. (I know this revelation is not finished. I truly believe I will be discovering more and more throughout eternity.) It was an amazing epiphany, revealing an entirely new insight into who God is, what Jesus did, the resident power of the Holy Spirit, and my identity from heaven's view. The cross changed everything between God and man. God went from visitation mode to habitation mode. No longer restrained to an occasional visit to mankind, God made a way to inhabit men. He did it by putting Himself in a human body to represent humanity and sacrificing Himself. He took my sin upon Himself, He took the punishment I deserved, and He killed my sin nature completely and exchanged it for His righteousness. And He did it without my help.

Sin is not an issue with God anymore. He is no longer dealing with sin. He has already dealt with it—all of it, for all humanity. The moment Jesus died, so did the sin He was carrying. My sin. Your sin. The sin of the entire world. The sin that separated man from God in the beginning was thoroughly annihilated. He carried my sin in His body on the cross. When He died, my sin died with Him. When He rose from death, I rose with Him as well as the same Spirit that caused His resurrection. My sin nature, however, stayed in the grave. It is dead. I am not about to resurrect it. Let's look at some scriptures about this. Romans 6:5–11 (NKJV) states:

> For if we have been united together in the likeness of His death, certainly we also shall be in the likeness of His resurrection, knowing this, that our old man was crucified with Him, that the body of sin might be done away with, that we should no longer be slaves of sin. For he who has died has been freed from sin. Now if we died with Christ, we believe that we shall also live with Him, knowing that Christ, having been raised from the dead, dies no more. Death no longer has dominion over Him. For the death that he died, He died to sin once for all; but the life that He lives, He lives to God. Likewise you also, reckon yourselves to be dead indeed to sin, but alive to God in Christ Jesus our Lord.

Every person on this planet is included in Jesus' sacrifice. Jesus has no do-overs. It is finished, one time for all men. Think about that for a few days or maybe months. We tend to put people in categories: good, better, best, worst, and all places in between. God has one category: the cross. An upcoming chapter in this book will explain this in depth. But for now, rest assured that I am not saying that I believe in universalism, unless universalism says that the cross of Jesus Christ is the only way to heaven. What I am saying is that Jesus' complete atonement included every person. Not all of us know it yet, and there is an escape clause. You can say no.

WHAT ABOUT THE WRATH OF GOD?

I hear a lot about the wrath of God. It is being preached from pulpits and street corners and over the Internet and the social media. From well-meaning people, I hear about sin and sin's consequences in my life. I understand that they are doing what they believe God wants them to do in the hope that people will think and repent. However, if I were listening to those words for the first time, I would not want a god whose demands are aggressive, and when they are not met, it is lethal.

Unfortunately, some believers have yet to believe. Many are of the opinion that God was personally offended by our sin. This required the death of His own Son to appease His anger. That mindset sounds very much like pagan religions. The gods are angry and must be appeased by innocent blood. Let me offer a question; what if Jesus' blood was not to pay off an angry God? It is the ultimate expression of love that redeems us from sin. The cross did not "satisfy" God's anger but His love.

In believing that God unloads wrath on sinners, people put their trust in their own self effort to avoid that scenario: their decisions, their faith, their repentance, and their works.

What if our salvation has nothing to do with us at all?

What if it is not your faith that cleanses you?

What if Jesus' mission was not to begin another religion called "Christianity," but to reveal and redeem God's image and likeness in human form? Jesus is what the Bible is all about, and you are what Jesus is all about.

Jesus did not die in order to condition God to love me, as if saying, "Someone has to pay for this!" God's love is unconditional. Some people love the argument that justice must be done. Yes, God is merciful, but He is also just, and it is His justice I need to look out for. They are right; His justice against the sin that was destroying His beloved creation was addressed and satisfied by the blood of Jesus. The blood of Jesus was not to appease the Father. He did not need it, I did. It was God's own blood, poured out for me. On the cross, Jesus was not changing God; He was changing me.

The atonement is much larger than I think. It reaches far beyond my comprehension. I see it the most when dealing with issues like this. I tend to have a need to figure everything out. If I can't, I will place God in a lovely box, tie it up with a pretty bow, and proclaim it understood. To assume that God thinks like I do is absurd. More than once I have heard Him say, *"I am bigger than you think I am. Trust me in this. I know what I am doing."*

There is an annual parade in the city I grew up. I love parades. This one happens to be the second largest floral parade in the United States. It is very well attended, so much so that some people bring tents and camp out on the sidewalks the night before the parade just to be assured of a good view. That has occurred to me, but we prefer option number two. We rise before the sun does, have lunch and snacks packed, and are ready to go. We bring chairs, blankets, sidewalk chalk and games for the little ones, and books for the older ones. Although the parade doesn't start until 10 a.m., we are there by 6 a.m., have found a good spot to watch, and settle in. Even at that hour, there are not many vacant places. The sidewalk is full of anticipation. You meet people, converse with total strangers, and have a great time waiting. When the road is closed to traffic, it is fair game. Many people take walks down the middle of the street, footballs are tossed, and chalk drawings are created. The place comes alive with activity.

Then I hear them coming, bullhorns and placards in tow, specific Bible verses memorized. From the way they present their message, I would not be surprised if they rehearsed in front of mirror. What is their message? It is all about God's anger and wrath toward sinners. The posters depict the fires of hell. Condemnation is the name; fear is the game. They shout in your face that if you are not "serving the Lord," then you can expect to go to hell when you die; which, by the way, could be at any moment. They quote damning scriptures, proclaiming that as truth. And they call it "the gospel." I would suggest that they read beyond the box they put their god in. They say Jesus Christ, but they do not preach Jesus Christ. God is love. End of discussion.

To God's heartache, there are people who reject His amazing offer; mostly because they don't know the God of the cross. Some have never heard it; some have listened to another gospel. Whatever the reason, they have said no. By doing so, they cannot experience all the cross has offered. In their lives, sin does exist, and it causes heartache, grief, and terrible consequences.

The god that is preached as severe and terrifying is not the God shown in the cross. It was there that a new covenant was made, clearly showing the heart God has for people. Pagan gods demand sacrifice. My God made the sacrifice Himself. Pagan gods threaten and terrify. Jesus Christ brings freedom from fear. He gives peace that cannot be described. The joy He gives is contagious.

I wonder what would happen if these well-meaning people would walk the street with gifts instead of ultimatums. What would happen if they would bring Kingdom life, hope, joy, love, peace, and even value to people? How wonderful would it be if, while walking the street and visiting the crowds, needs were met, people were healed, hope was disbursed, and the gospel was presented in truth? After all, it is good news!

BE HOLY, FOR I AM HOLY

God's wrath was poured out on Jesus at Calvary. It was not wrath against men, nor was it anger against Jesus. It was wrath against sin. Graham Cooke says, "When God looks at you, He sees nothing wrong with you. He only sees what is missing in your experience with Him."

"How can this be? I know myself. I blow it all the time. No matter how hard I try, I will never be holy." Are statements like that running through your mind? I learned something so magnificent that it changed my struggle forever. In 1 Peter 1:15–16, the author quoted an Old Testament prophet, who spoke for God, "*Be holy, for I am holy.*" I want to show you an amazing truth, but you will need to use your imagination. Are you ready?

I picture God standing before me with a beautiful gift in His hands. Reaching out for me to take it, He says, *"Be holy, for I am holy. This is My holiness. I am giving My holiness to you. Here it is; take it and be filled with My holiness."* What is happening? There is no way I can manufacture by my own efforts what God wants to simply give me. It is His holiness I carry. It is His righteousness in me. The law says, "Do!" Grace says, "Done!"

Jesus did it all for me. He took my sin, and replaced it with His righteousness. How important is this to understand? Anything less is not the gospel. Self-improvement methods and behavior modification days are over. I am, very literally, God's righteousness. Why would I to try to add to that? It is complete. It is enough. It is finished.

IF GOD IS NOT DEALING WITH MY SIN . . .

If God is no longer dealing with sin; if He had finished that work on the cross, what is He doing in me? What does God want from me now? When all I knew had been about disciplining and chastisement, what replaces those methods in my life? How will I keep the faith if I don't have to work at it?

I have an answer to that question. God is no longer sin-conscience. The sin issue has been dealt with successfully. God sees me in Christ; He is totally focused on my righteousness. That is what I have learned to expect from Him. He no longer thinks in terms of my sin, and He is committed to establishing my righteousness. To think this way may take some practice.

I begin to change my focus; God is now establishing His righteousness in me. I went from works *for* righteousness to works *of* righteousness. I cannot produce God's fruit; the Holy Spirit produces His fruit through me.

I am filled with anticipation for the next revelation from the Holy Spirit, teaching me who God really is. I no longer tell God about my sin; I tell sin about my God. He is teaching me how to live out my new identity. He is teaching me everything new. By agreeing with God, learning how He sees me, and walking in His ever-present grace, I literally walk out of sin-consciousness and into His holiness. I have closed the door to my past. The sin nature I used to carry is dead. The old issues I used to struggle with constantly have absolutely no place in my life now. Today and all of my tomorrows are filled with anticipation, learning how to walk in newness of life.

I have gone from living past-present to living present-future.

Today I am eager to understand the truth of the gospel and how that affects my life. My name has changed to "saint"; my game plan has changed to grace. I get to partner with Holy Spirit (my BFF) in forming me into the image of Jesus. I know my identity in Christ, and I am learning my purpose in His kingdom. That is the key to transformation.

How does that work? First, I had to know that, in God's eyes and because of the cross, I am no longer a sinner. I must know that Jesus changed me from sinner to saint. If I try to build on anything other than the truth of what Jesus actually accomplished, it will crumble under the weight of religious ritual and my own effort. I used to be constantly worried about the sin in my life and was quick to point out the sin in other people. Friends, that is not freedom; it is bondage. It may be presented as gospel, but it is not the gospel of Jesus Christ. I cannot get rid of a negative by focusing on it.

The Apostle Paul, in his letter to the church in Galatia, addresses this problem.

I marvel that you are turning away so soon from Him who called you in the grace of Christ; to a different gospel, which is not another; but there are some who trouble you and want to pervert the gospel of Christ. (Galatians 1:6)

This only I want to learn from you: Did you receive the Spirit by the works of the law, or by the hearing of faith? Are you so foolish? Having begun in the Spirit, are you now being made perfect by the flesh? (Galatians 3:2–3)

Good question. Perhaps I should look at the result of the cross again, this time from the Mirror Bible:

We were like seeds planted together in the same soil, to be co-quickened to life. If we were included in His death we are equally included in His resurrection. We perceive that our old lifestyle was co-crucified together with Him; this concludes that the vehicle that accommodated sin in us was scrapped and rendered entirely useless. Our slavery to sin has come to an end. If nothing else stops you from doing something wrong, death certainly does. Faith sees us joined in His death and alive with Him in His resurrection. It is plain for all to see that death lost its dominion over Christ in His resurrection; He need not ever die again to prove a further point. His appointment with death was once-off. As far as sin is concerned, He is dead. The reason for His death was to take away the sin of the world; His life now exhibits our union with the life of God. This reasoning is equally relevant to you. Calculate the cross; there can only be one logical conclusion: He died your death; that means you died unto sin, and are now alive unto God. Sin-consciousness can never again feature in your future! You are in Christ Jesus; His Lordship is the authority of this union. (Romans 6:5–11)

I believe what God's Word says is truth. From that point I can proceed in the life He has already secured for me, checking everything by His Word, always asking for understanding. So often religion has covered the truth with so much fear that many are caught in its trap. I truly understand that situation. I lived it for decades until God set me free.

Living in that freedom is really easy. So many believe Christianity is very difficult. They think that the life of faith is one struggle after another: two steps forward, three steps back. I feel so sorry for them. They are still stuck in performance mode. In that world people never reach their goal simply because the outcome depends entirely on their works. They don't know the God of grace.

Basically, it is a minute-by-minute tuning in to His voice and then acting on what He says. It is worked out by changes in my thinking about God, myself, and those around me. My mind turns from negative thinking to Kingdom possibilities. It is worked out by changing my words from what I have to do, to what God is doing in and through my life. Again in Romans 12, Paul describes this as "renewing my mind." Learning to think what God thinks.

Grace is not the beginning point in my life. Grace is the entire point. It is not only the foundation, it is the entire structure. All of life is enveloped in grace. Everything holy and righteous flows out of grace. Grace is not a thread, weaving its way through the tapestry of life; it is the entire picture.

Grace is the bottom line of all the beautiful, powerful, and amazing superlatives about God becoming reality for me. God's rich love, His abundant mercy, His relentless kindness, His might and power, His majesty, His glory, His favor—all the attributes that leave us overwhelmed with gratitude and wonder—are rolled up in grace and worked out in our lives. Grace is where the rubber meets the road and enables us to live heaven to earth.

There is enough grace over me at this moment to last several lifetimes. I may miss the mark from time to time, but when I do, I train my thoughts to go directly to His truth. No matter how often I need to, I take the thought that did not originate in heaven, and with the understanding that I have already been declared righteous because of Jesus, bring it right back to the cross where I was declared righteous. I praise God for His forgiveness and keep going. It is His grace that gives us the power to keep going. It is grace that makes us want to stay in God's presence all day, every day. Grace does not excuse sin; it compels us to let Jesus live His life through us.

I cannot live the Christian life. Only Jesus can live it through me.

When the truth of the gospel began to wrap around me and I discovered God's amazing grace, I have never be the same. I went from religion to passion. When I began to understand the depth of God's love for me, all I desired was to love Him back and to share that love with everyone I know. "It is finished!" Those words have changed my life forever. But it doesn't end there. As I pondered and thought about what I had learned, I had questions. (Of course I did—that's what I do!) Thrilled and eager to learn more I had to find out about the process.

THE PROCESS

There must be a process. There is always a process. That is how we get from point A to point Z. When I asked about it, "The process," answered Holy Spirit, "is discovering what God has already deposited within you. It grows from glory to glory. I will reveal truth about Jesus, about the Father, and about His plan for you. *The process is one of growing discoveries that bring stunning encounters for your future and for what God had in mind when He created you.* The word for you, Wild Thing, is adventure." And so it has been and will ever be.

Walking with the Lord is just plain fun. One of the adventures I encountered right after this revelation was about a binder. Not an unusual binder, just a plain white one, that happened to contain journals, notes, and teachings I had collected over several years.

I had just volunteered to lead a Bible study. The date was set, invitations mailed, the event announced, and I was beginning to prepare. I had planned to use the white binder with all of those wonderful scriptures, illustrations, and everything I needed for this project. I looked everywhere for it. My husband joined me in the hunt for the white binder. It was hiding somewhere, I am sure, but wherever it was, I was not finding it. We tore the house apart. No binder. The date was coming up soon, and the source I intended to depend on was nowhere to be found. I was beginning to panic. *"Lord, I have looked everywhere for that binder. Please help! I can't find it anywhere!"* His answer was amusing. He simply said, with a happy smile, *"Yeah, I know!"* Oh great! I could see how this was going to proceed. He wanted to give me fresh truth, new life, and new insight to share.

It can be more than a little disconcerting when I don't feel fully prepared. I surely did not want to see faces around my dining room table, waiting for something that was not going to happen. Prayer takes on an entirely new dimension in this kind of situation. I felt myself feeling an exhilarating combination of excitement and trepidation. By this time in my life, I certainly did not want to share something just because I was on the docket. If it was not from God, I did not want to do it. Sitting by a fire pit one evening as I was voicing my concern, I heard the Lord say, *"Don't worry. You are complete in Me. You will have what you need, and you will share it with complete understanding."*

I am complete in Christ. As I sat by the fire, the immense meaning of those words began to fill my mind. It has immeasurable possibilities. Each one giving a wonderful perspective about God and about my identity in Him. Every month since has been like that.

Today, ten years later, as we meet together, the people are bringing their own epiphany from the throne room. It has been so remarkable to see us all change into His likeness. Each person is astonished at how God loves to become a vital part of our lives. Personally it is thrilling; corporately it is dynamic.

BOSS/WORKER OR BODY?

It was during one of the studies around my table that I was given a brilliant picture about my identity in Christ. I had always considered myself a worker for the Lord, thinking it was sort of like a boss–worker relationship, much like life in the military. "Yes, Sir. I am here at Your command." Even as a child I thrilled to the song, "I'm in the Lord's Army!" It was part of my identity as a Christian. God is Boss; I am worker.

As I was looking around the table, Holy Spirit began to show me how God sees the church—not as boss/worker, but as His Body on the earth. The more I contemplated the differences, the bigger they became.

Boss	Worker
Separate identities.	One identity.
Separate roles to play.	One purpose.
Separate mindsets.	One mind.
Different value put on performance.	Invaluable, Irreplaceable.
Has a job to do.	Has a life to live.
Focused on performance.	Focused on being part of Jesus.

I am part of Jesus' body on this earth. God did not make a way for me to act like Jesus, but to be like Jesus.

FREEDOM

One day at church, we sang a rousing song about freedom. I heard that familiar voice ask me a question: *"What do you want to be free from?"* Do you mean it, Lord? I thought about it all through the service. By the end of church that day, I had come to a conclusion: I wanted to be free from *me*. Free from the tyranny of *me*. Free from the demands I put on myself and on others. Free to be all God sees me to be. I felt like I could fly. I flew through the day and into the next. Then it hit me. I would discover how much bondage I was in. A bondage of my own making, too.

It was during the two years my mother-in-law lived with us.

I was in awe of her from the first time we met. A sweeter woman would be difficult to find. I wanted to serve her in any way I could to make her life easier. She had a form of Parkinson's disease. It had not progressed far, and there wasn't much she could not do. However, when she heard the word "Parkinson," she simply decided she was an invalid. Even though she was well able, she wanted someone to do everything for her, except maybe to chew. If she had thought of that one, I'm sure she would have found a way.

Suddenly I became aware of a monster in the house. It had my face. Everything irritated me. Every few minutes, she wanted my full attention. I was full of anger, mostly because Mom refused to help herself. I was determined to do everything humanly possible to serve her, but my dream of being free from *me* came crashing down. It took all my strength, plus much help from Holy Spirit, to keep my emotions under control. I saw just how free from me I wasn't. What do you do in a situation like that? I refused to cause her pain in any way and would not cause stress in the house. Putting this situation squarely in my newfound freedom in Christ, I needed to know how to stay free from the desire in me to run screaming into the night.

I made some significant discoveries. First, the struggle is not sin; it is a struggle. Being part of this world, struggles happen. What am I supposed to do? Pretend the struggle doesn't exist? No, that is stupid. The struggle was real. So was my attitude, even though I had kept it under control.

How does a person handle this situation? The answer isn't ultra-spiritual or saintly. Just keep on walking. Keep on doing the right things. Even when feelings are utterly contrary. I felt like a guppy taking on a Poseidon-strength tsunami. I didn't need to ask for direction about what the right thing to do was. I knew that. So, I kept walking as God said I already was: righteous, holy, blameless, and above reproach. The result? I won a huge battle: the one raging in my mind. My enemy could not find place to hook me. He could not find a foothold anywhere. I was free!

WALKING IN GRACE

Walking in grace means that I have no confidence in the flesh. Coming from one who put all faith in my works, that statement brought it all together for me. Instead, it is the process of discovering who God is in me. Grace means constantly growing in greater revelation of the fullness of God who is already there. It is the process of recognizing the full measure of the Holy Spirit who resides in me.

Living in the grace zone is living from an entirely new frame of reference. Imagine the possibilities! God sees every one as finished.

For consideration:

Imagine what life would be like when I am completely free from requirements, whether they are ones made for myself or ones expected from others?

What is included in the statement Jesus made when He said "It is finished"?

The possibilities are almost beyond imagination, endless provision from God's throne for everything life brings. Bring it home; what does it mean for you?

What, if any, thoughts and beliefs will I want to change in light of God's true picture of the atoning work of Jesus?

Can I embrace what God has been waiting for me to acknowledge?

It's okay. Go ahead and ask Him.

CHAPTER 7

CLOSE ENCOUNTERS

Incarnation means God in the flesh. An accurate understanding of this is extremely significant. It will affect every other perception regarding my life with God. As vital as my understanding of what Jesus did, is the comprehension of who Jesus is. They are one and the same. To understand the gospel, I need to know that those two concepts cannot be separated.

I became so focused on what must be "done" to be saved that I missed who Jesus is. The union of God and man in the person of Jesus Christ is the heart of the gospel. That union existed in heaven and then continued on earth. Its influence is becoming more and more obvious to me. I see it in religious theory about spirituality and the natural world. Often, religious circles fear anything that has to do with creation itself. If an issue is not totally spiritual, it is to be avoided because of the belief that the natural world is associated with evil.

Separation is at the core of this concept. The belief begins with the idea that God separated Himself from mankind; therefore, man needs to make every effort to bridge that separation. It all boils down to the ancient belief that because of God's holiness, He cannot associate with man.

In the early church, it became so prevalent that John called it the spirit of antichrist. These people were teaching that because Jesus was God, He could not have been a man. Spirit and natural will never mix; they are poles apart. So what did they do with Jesus, God in the flesh? Their belief was that Jesus came to earth in spirit form only. When He appeared to men, they saw His spirit, not a human body. That is who

John is addressing when he wrote that the fact that God became flesh is vital; to reject this is to fall into demonic influence.

I have to wonder how they nailed a spirit to the cross.

The same lie that John fought exists today. The church has adopted the idea that God is far away, unreachable. Therefore, if we want to know Him we must find a way to do it ourselves. The result is centuries of religious do's and don'ts; what to do to find God and what will send Him away. The underlying message is that natural and spiritual cannot co-exist. The farther I go with that line of thought, the farther away God becomes, which, in turn forces me to create methods to find Him.

My enemy does not want me to know that God so loved the world, that He entered it Himself as human to remove the sin that separated me from Him and to reinstate His original design for mankind.

Most people believe that when Jesus came to earth, it was almost like Jesus, the man, and Jesus, God's Son were somehow glued together while on the earth. Yes, Jesus laid down His divine power and privilege, but they were not gone; they were set aside. All the power of the Godhead was resident in Jesus. I don't know of any other person who spoke to storms, and they obeyed. As far as I know, Jesus was the first man to actually walk on water or speak life into a man who had been dead for four days. Wherever He went, miracles followed—so many they could not be counted.

The truth is, the incarnation makes mincemeat of every effort I can make to approach God.

One of the most compelling Scriptures about Jesus' identity is found in the gospel of John. John begins with an amazing description of who Jesus was.

> In the beginning was the Word, and the Word was with God, and the Word was God. He was in the beginning with God. All things were made through Him, and without Him nothing was made that was made. . . . .And the Word became flesh and dwelt among us, and we beheld His glory, the glory as of the only begotten of the Father, full of grace and truth. . . . And of His fullness we have all received, and grace for grace. For

the law was given through Moses, but grace and truth
came through Jesus Christ. (John 1:1–3, 14; NKJV):

John spoke of Jesus, who was God Himself. Suddenly the invisible
eternal Word takes on visible form! John saw His glory.

Jesus' divinity can never be separated from His humanity. Christ
as God and Christ as man—there was never a separation between God
the Father and God the Son. We have been obsessed about a separation
that doesn't exist in God's mind. Many people believe that Jesus was a
man who was inhabited with the Holy Spirit, nothing more. A seemingly insignificant change in what we believe becomes a monumental
blockage to the powerful truth. Jesus' message to the people He encountered was that God's kingdom had come to earth. Jesus, God with skin
on, lived, carried, and dispersed heaven's reality on the earth.

Yes, as a man Jesus experienced all things human. As a man, Jesus
lived a perfect example for us; He was a man who was completely and
thoroughly filled with God's Spirit. As God, Jesus brought the divine
into the natural world. Heaven's realities brought to earth's situations.
The most significant piece of this belief is that, as Jesus was, so are we
in this world. First John 4:17 (NKJV) states: *Love has been perfected
among us in this: that we may have boldness in the day of judgment;
because as He is, so are we in this world.*

That, my friends, is the point of the gospel.

Colossians 1:17 says, "In Christ all things hold together." I have
noticed that the closer I feel God is to me, the more I see Him everywhere. John 1:3 states, "All things came into being by Him, and apart
from Him nothing came into being that has come into being."

What part of our existence is secular and devoid of the life of the
Trinity? What part of our life does not include God? By being in Christ,
His kingdom goes wherever we go.

As awesome as that is, the beauty of the incarnation is that it doesn't
stop there. Because of the incarnation, I am brought into the exact same
unity Jesus and the Father enjoy. Because Jesus represented humanity,
I am included in the Divine relationship between Father, Son, and
Holy Spirit. God's heart of reconciliation is proven by my inclusion in
Christ. The reconciliation that culminated at Calvary began before the

foundation of the earth. God saw me in Christ before creation. In His mind, it was finished long before I was created.

Read in the Mirror Bible:

> It is in Christ that God finds an accurate and complete expression of Himself, in a human body! (While the expanse cannot measure or define God, His exact likeness is displayed in human form. Jesus proves that human life is tailor-made for God!) Jesus mirrors our completeness and endorses our true identity. He is "I AM" in us. (Colossians 2:9–10)

> In Him the image and likeness of God is made visible in human life in order that every one may recognize their true origin in Him. He is the firstborn of every creature. (What darkness veiled from us He unveiled. In Him we clearly see the mirror reflection of our original life. The Son of His love gives accurate evidence of His image in human form. God can never again be invisible!) (Colossians 1:15)

> The days of window-shopping are over! In Him every face is unveiled. In gazing with wonder at the blueprint likeness of God displayed in human form, we suddenly realize that we are looking at ourselves! Every feature of His image in mirrored in us! This is the most radical transformation engineered by the Spirit of the Lord. (2 Corinthians 3:18)

This is incarnation in its fullness. God included mankind. I am literally Jesus' body on the earth today. Just by living out my days, the Kingdom of God is being established. I don't have to work at it; I simply live it.

LENS CHANGES

These concepts required me to see things differently. Believe it or not, things look different from God's point of view. I have had countless lens changes in my life. The Holy Spirit shows me something that gives me a completely new view of a subject—a heavenly view.

I love the lens change that occurred in the life of Peter. It is recorded in Acts, chapter ten. This experience completely reshaped the way he believed. God showed Peter His truth; something that had never occurred to him before.

At this time in his life, Peter was the pastor of the church in Jerusalem. He was the leader of thousands of believers, had great influence, and needed a lens change!

Visiting a friend named Simon, Peter took some time alone to pray on the rooftop. It was around noon, and Peter was getting hungry. God was about to change something Peter considered an absolute, set-in-stone tradition, passed down through the centuries. As he looked into the sky, he had a vision that would threaten any ordinary man to run for the hills. Coming toward him was what looked like a large sheet, full of food that was absolutely forbidden in Jewish culture. If that was not enough, the sheet was accompanied by a voice telling Peter to "rise, kill, and eat."

What? This was incredulous! Not me! I never have, nor will I eat something that is forbidden. I am a good Jewish boy! Unbelievable!

I can only imagine what some acquaintances of mine would be doing after an experience like that. Most likely rebuking the devil for putting such temptation in front of them. Not only were Jews forbidden to eat these foods, they couldn't even touch them.

It took this same scenario three times to get through to Peter. The clincher was when God told him, "What God has cleansed, don't you call unclean, or common, or untouchable." Major lens change, Peter. Little did Peter know that something wonderful was in the works.

While Peter was scratching his head over this, God had been preparing someone the Jews would never consider associating with. His name was Cornelius. He was a Gentile (problem number one), and he was a Roman soldier (problem number two—through infinity).

What did God see in Cornelius? Not a usual man, to be sure. He was a devout man, a man who prayed to God and led his entire household to do the same. Cornelius was generous, contributing to the needs of others. He had a heart after God, even before he knew about Jesus. Imagine! That thought alone can send some people running for the prayer circle to pray for deliverance.

What is spectacular is that this Gentile, this Roman soldier, this one considered unworthy, was visited by an angel. Now this is stretching things way out of our comfort zone. I have learned that God can do whatever He wants to do, without my approval. The angelic visitor gave Cornelius specific instructions where to find Peter. When located, Peter was to come back for a visit (another forbidden subject, by the way).

Let's get this straight. Peter had a collision with heaven that challenged his entire belief system. Thankfully he was up to the challenge, and because of his obedience, the gospel was opened up for Gentiles.

I have come to look forward to lens changes in my walk with the Lord. It always opens up a whole new universe of possibilities.

The apostle Paul also had a life-changing encounter with Jesus. Totally believing that he was serving God's purposes, his mission was to collect and imprison people of this new sect called Christianity. They were a threat to what he believed to be the only truth.

Detailed mission from the authorities in hand, Paul, then called Saul, was on his way to Damascus to arrest and stop Christians in the area. He was absolutely positive about his view on the subject. Nothing on earth could persuade him otherwise.

On the way to his destination, he had a God-encounter that changed the course of history. God had different plans for Paul. How could one, so focused on what he believed to be truth, do a 180-degree turn in the opposite direction? Simple. He was introduced to Jesus.

Paul, the golden-haired boy that the powers that be put all their trust in to fulfill their mission, was derailed and detained on his way. Paul, the one with all the knowledge and training in leadership, was suddenly faced with a truth that he could not deny. The truth was that Jesus Christ was God's Son. He came to earth as a man to redeem mankind back to God. By so doing, Jesus eliminated all other roads to God, including the one Paul had dedicated his life to defend and protect.

Jesus came to Paul in a light so bright that it knocked him off his horse and blinded him for several days. He had to be led to a nearby town where he sat alone with his thoughts, confronted with the truth and his own actions against the truth. I am sure those few days were filled with unbelievable trauma, mind-altering concepts, and revelation about who Jesus really is.

But much more than that, Paul understood the gospel in ways that no other man had. He understood grace. There was no trace of confidence in anything but Jesus and Him crucified. The years that followed were filled with revelation about God's love, His purposes, and His methods; the deep things of God were revealed to Paul who, in turn, passed on those truths to all who would follow.

Paul had a lens change that, as it turns out, changed the way I see the gospel, too.

EPIPHANY

I am to the point where my lens changes fill me with anticipation. Nothing is more exciting than when the Holy Spirit shares some heavenly information with me.

Allow me to share an experience that sent this perspective home to me. I was attending a woman's conference several years ago. It was thrilling and exciting being among like-minded people who were all focused on worship and God's Word.

For some reason, I had just been through something disturbing and couldn't drag myself into the spirit of the evening. I was standing as far back in the corner of the room as one could get, feeling frustrated, angry, and not at all spiritual in any sense of the word. I knew how to get myself out of the funk I was in, but I just didn't want to yet. The worship was wonderful, so I decided to be a big girl and get over myself. I began to worship, on the outside, anyway. It didn't change how I was feeling, but I believed there are only two times to praise the Lord: when you feel like it and when you don't. So, as a step of faith I joined in.

Moments later, in my imagination (my mind, where the Holy Spirit often mingles with me), I saw Jesus walking toward me. He spoke one short sentence that melted away all the negatives I was feeling: *"May I have this dance?"* The One who loves me beyond comprehension asked me to join Him in the worship. Of course!

The next night, I was over my attitude, and this time I found a seat close to the front. I didn't need to force myself to join in this time, and during the same song, I saw Jesus coming toward me again. The same thing happened and much more.

As we were dancing (again, in my mind/spirit), Jesus looked at me with such joy and delight, threw His head back and laughed as if I was His reason to live. Again, we began dancing. Within a few moments we merged as one person. We went from dancing partners to one person, and danced around the room. I saw Jesus reach out and touch someone. It was His hand, but it was my hand, too. Around the room we went, touching many people; His hand reaching out, my hand reaching out, we were one. I was in Him, and He was in me. Every time we reached to touch someone, He would say, *"Dance with Me . . . dance with Me . . . dance with Me through life. Dance with Me."*

What was happening? God was showing me that it is His life in me that does the work. Yes, I am moving in and with Him, but His power was being dispersed through me. I was simply a vessel, a much-honored one to be part of the dance.

HAVE ANOTHER THOUGHT

Much is being said about our responsibilities as Christians. I fully endorse that thought, although I prefer to think of it as a purpose instead of a responsibility, simply because responsibilities can quickly turn into works.

When I find myself stuck in a place, and am having difficulty finding my way out, Holy Spirit whispers to me, "Have another thought. *What does God see in this situation?* What do things look like from His point of view? Then ask Him what He thinks about it. Make that answer your thought. Engage with His reality." When I identify with God, I see myself as He sees me. When I practice that lifestyle, transformation takes place.

Paul had a solution for getting unstuck. Actually, it is a very simple one. It has been called "inner healing," or "a cleansing process"; Paul called it renewing the mind. Where lens changing has to do with seeing things from God's viewpoint, renewing my mind is the process of learning to think like God thinks. From that point I find that so much changes. My thought life changes, and my language soon follows. I not only have the mind of Christ, I also speak what I hear Him speak. You will find it in Romans 12:1–2 (THE MIRROR BIBLE):

> Live consistent with who you really are, inspired by the loving kindness of God. My brothers, the most practical expression of worship is to make your bodies available to Him as a living sacrifice; this pleases Him more than any religious routine. He desires to find visible, individual expression in your person. Do not allow current religious tradition to mold you into its pattern of reasoning. Like an inspired artist, give attention to the detail of God's desire to find expression in you. Become acquainted with perfection. To accommodate yourself to the delight and good pleasure of Him who will transform your thoughts afresh from within.

IDENTITY: KEY TO TRANSFORMATION

Desire the new enough to let go of the old. In Christ Jesus, newness is all I have. The old is dead and gone, done away with by Jesus Himself on the cross. I have good news! When Jesus rose from the grave, my old sin nature did not. Now every day, every moment, is a new me to discover. The question to ask is, how does God see me? Life becomes the adventure of learning to become who God sees me to be in Christ.

What an adventure that is! I happen to have an imagination that matches any Hollywood writer or director. Within sixty seconds, one single thought can become an all-out Cecil B. DeMille production, complete with technicolor, surround sound, and a cast of thousands. An imagination like that can be a gift and a challenge at the same time.

One of my favorite sayings is: "If you want to make a mountain out of a molehill, you have to move a lot of dirt!" Welcome to Murphy Excavation Service. Although by nature I trend to lean toward "Pollyanna syndrome," there are times when I start down a negative thought path, realizing only after my emotions are full-blown; (sound effects, 3-D, the works), that I could have stopped the whole drama from the start by practicing these very simple steps.

Being very tired of back-peddling my thoughts out of a pit, I began to deliberately remember who I am in Christ.

> Therefore, if any of you have been raised up with Christ, keep seeking the things above where Christ is seated at the right hand of God. Set your mind on things above, not on things that are on the earth, for you have died and your life is hidden with Christ in God. (Colossians 3:1)

Listen to those verses from the Mirror Bible:

> See yourselves co-raised with Christ! Now ponder with persuasion the consequence of your co-inclusion in Him. Relocate yourselves mentally! Engage your thoughts with throne room realities where you are co-seated with Christ in the executive authority of God's right hand.

But what about times when I don't make the grade? What happens when mistakes are made? Take a look at 1 John 1:7. It may be a wonderful, new thought: "If we walk in the light as He is in the light, we have fellowship with one another, and the blood of Jesus Christ His Son cleanses us from all sin." The word *cleanses* here is in perfect-present tense. That means that we have been cleansed, we are cleansed, and we will be cleansed. The fact that Jesus' blood has already cleansed us from all sin, is cleansing us from all sin, and will cleanse us from all sin, all at the same time. When I make a mistake or miss the mark, I recognize it, and thank the Lord that it has already been forgiven. It is forgiven today, and tomorrow's mistakes are forgiven as well. I am free from the heavy burden of perfection, knowing that day-by-day, the Holy Spirit is perfecting the image of Jesus in me.

IDENTITY SCRIPTURES: Just a few to think about.

What I do does not determine who I am; who I am determines what I do.

In Christ I am:

Matthew 5:13-14—the salt of the earth, light

John 1:12—A child of God

15:1, 5—connected to the vine, a channel of God's life

15:16—chosen by God, appointed to bear fruit

Romans 5:1— justified, completely and totally forgiven and made righteous

6:1-6—died with Christ and to the power of sin's rule

6:18—slave of righteousness

8:1—forever free from condemnation

8:14-15; Galatians 3:26, 4:6—God is my Father

8:17—a joint heir with Christ, sharing in Jesus' inheritance

1 Corinthians 2:16— given the mind of Christ

3:16; 6:9— temple, dwelling place of God. His Spirit, His life lives in me.

6:17—united with the Lord, one spirit with Him

6:19-20—bought with a price, I am not my own. I belong to God.

12:27; Ephesians 5:30—member of Christ's body

2 Corinthians 1:21; Ephesians 1:13–14—established, anointed, and sealed by Holy Spirit

5:18–19—reconciled to God, and a minister of reconciliation

5:21—the righteousness of God in Christ

Ephesians 1:5— blessed with every spiritual blessing

2:6—seated with Christ in the heavenlies

2:10—God's workmanship, His handiwork

2:18—direct access to God by the Holy Spirit

3:12—approach God with confidence, freedom and boldness

4:24—righteous and holy

Philippians 3:20, Ephesians 2:6—citizen of heaven, of God's kingdom, seated today in heaven

Colossians 1:14—the debt against me has been cancelled

2:10—complete in Christ

3:3—hidden with Christ in God

3:12; 1 Thessalonians 1:4—chosen of God, holy and dearly loved

1 Thessalonians 5:5—child of light, not of darkness

2 Timothy 1:7—given a spirit of power, love, and sound mind

1 Peter 1:4—given exceedingly great and precious promises by God, and am a partaker of God's divine nature.

1 Peter 2:9–10—royal priest, a holy nation, God's own possession

1 John 5:18—born of God. The evil one cannot touch me

I'VE BEEN MORPHED!

Literally everything in life becomes about one thing—being made in the image of God.

What if—every situation comes with the knowledge of what God sees it to be?

What if—every question is answered by viewing it through the lens of grace?

What if—God is not working on my behavior? He is creating my identity in Jesus.

What if—I do not deal with the old self? Instead, I lay it aside. I bury it. It no longer has any effect on my life.

So much is taught about behavior modification, as if I can change myself. I may be able to make a little progress, but soon discover that I am back where I started. Great honor is given to the self-made man, and truthfully, there are those who are gifted and perform wonderful acts of benevolence to the world. Even these people did not work on their own, whether they give credit to God or not. The majority of men have the intention to pull themselves up by their own bootstraps, and applause is their reward. If the truth were seen, a self-made man is proof positive of poor workmanship. God has placed a divine spark of creativity in many wonderful people. Some have run with it, but none can really call it their own.

The sorry message that it is a constant thing to fall short of God's perfection is being preached every week. There have been countless Sundays I have left the church feeling discouraged and worthless because I have been reminded over and over that I am not good enough.

I have to ask—not good enough for whom? Who is the judge that pronounces judgment on me? Is it the studied, well-rehearsed clergy who can judge? Perhaps it is those who have been where I am and since reached another level of goodness. During a conversation about judging the behavior of others, I once asked the one passing judgment to look at their hands. When they did, I asked them a question: "Do you see any nail-print scars? If not, please don't put yourself in the place that only One can possess." If I remember right, the discussion ended abruptly.

God sees beyond what I see. God sees me based on what Jesus has done. That is the only way He sees me, and He has seen me in that perspective long before I was born.

In John 12:31–33, Jesus told people the reason He came to the earth. We have heard these verses often, but perhaps we can look at them in a different light: "Now is the judgment of this world; now the ruler of this world will be cast out. And I, if I am lifted up from the earth, will draw all people to Myself. This He said, signifying by what death He would die."

Jesus spoke about making judgments. He said, now is the time that the world will be judged—now, not some time in the future, but now. Then He told them that now, the time He was on the earth, the ruler of the world will be cast out. Great! That is good news! He speaks further about judgment in the next two verses: "*And I, if I am lifted up from the earth* (meaning crucifixion) *will draw all men to Myself.*" This is where I made an amazing discovery. The words *men*, or *peoples*, given here, are not in the original text. They were added by translators. I believe Jesus was not speaking of people here, but of judgment.

Let's look at that statement without those words: If I am lifted up from the earth I will draw all to Myself. All what? What is Jesus' topic of discussion? Judgment. If I am lifted up, I will draw all judgment to Myself. How much judgment? All judgment. What does this mean? Jesus, on the cross, took the judgment of every human, past, present, and future, onto Himself. He also took the sin of every human, past, present and future, and removed it as far as the east is from the west. And it was finished before the foundation of the earth.

DID YOU KNOW?

Did you know? I read those words often in Paul's letters. There are many things I have yet to learn.

For many years I did not know that my redemption was finished in God's mind before the foundation of the earth. That magnificent truth is found in several scriptures:

> All who dwell on the earth will worship Him, whose names have not been written in the Book of Life of the Lamb slain from the foundation of the world. And those who dwell on the earth will marvel, whose names are not written in the Book of Life from the foundation of the world. (Revelation 13:7–8)

> Ephesians 1:3–4–
> Blessed be the God and Father of our Lord Jesus Christ, who has blessed us with every spiritual blessing in the heavenly places in Christ, just as He chose us in Him before the foundation of the *world, that we should be holy and without blame before Him.*

Speaking of the rest believers have because of the redemptive work of Jesus:

> Hebrews 4:3—
> "For we who have believed enter that rest, as He has said; "So I swore in my wrath, they shall not enter my rest," although the works were finished from the foundation of the world."

2 Timothy 1:9:
Who has saved us and called us with a holy calling, not according to our works, but according to His own purpose and grace which was given to us in Christ Jesus before time began.

Titus 1:2–
In hope of eternal life which God, who cannot lie, promised before time began.

1 Peter 1:20–
He indeed was foreordained before the foundation of the world, but was manifest in these last times for you...

Why is this so vital to understand? It shows me that God had me in His heart and mind before He said, "Let there be light." God found me in Jesus before He lost me in Adam.

My identity is intimately intertwined with Jesus.

Paul states in Romans 8:28–32
And we know that all things work together for good to those who love God, to those who are the called according to His purpose For whom He foreknew, He also predestined to be conformed to the image of His Son, that He might be the firstborn among many brethren. Moreover whom He predestined, these He also called; whom He called, these He also justified; and whom He justified, these He also glorified. What then shall we say to these things? If God is for us, who can be against us? He who did not spare His own Son, but delivered Him up for us all, how shall He not with Him freely give us all things?

How vital is it to understand our identity in Christ? I'll let you answer that yourself.

Remember, God loves to work in you; He loves to work with you. He loves to give you understanding of your identity as He sees you. He desires that you partner with Him in this life, fulfilling the great purposes He sees for you. Can you believe that?

It seems too good to be true. That's how I know it is God.

CHAPTER 8
NEW NORMAL

Constant change is here to stay. The challenge for believers is to keep the changes positive. I heard Graham Cooke at a conference, say that it is one battle to take the land, and it is another to keep it. For me, the key is to remember this fact when in the heat of battle.

Often I have a God-encounter and then go from that experience to face the same issues I have always faced, giving the same responses I have always given. Yes, my God encounter was real; now I need to learn to bring that experience into everyday living. It is called practice. I have to practice walking out what I have learned until it is solid in my mind and heart, and its fruit is being produced in my life until my responses are consistently aligned with God's purposes.

The process is about discovering what God has already placed in me. Every discovery comes with an opportunity to put it to the test—or work it out as I move through my day. I can be sure that God will supply plenty of occasions for me to practice what I am learning.

Sometimes my "forgetter" works better than my "rememberer." I may find myself halfway down the path of my old ways of responding to situations before I remember that I have something much better available to me. It is never too late to make U-turns. I remember I have grace; I am covered!

I heard a beautiful illustration about this. When Noah and his family were inside the ark, waves and winds were tossing it around like a beach ball on the ocean. I'm sure Noah slipped and fell more than once during that tumultuous time. Even if he did, he was still protected from the storm and from God's wrath. Outside of the ark was mass destruction. But Noah and his family were covered, protected, and safe inside the ark. It is the same with grace. I am covered, protected, and safe, even when I slip and fall. Is God's merciful love so thin that I am not secure in it? No, I think not.

THE FAITH FACTOR

From the first moment until the last, faith will always be a major part of my relationship with God. To some, it is the only factor. To others, it is confusing. To many it is plain frustrating. Whatever I have learned about the subject of faith, it will be in my face every day in some way. I don't claim to know everything about faith, but I can share what I have learned thus far.

Hebrews 11:1 states: *"Now faith is the substance of things hoped for, the evidence of things not seen."* Has that verse confused anyone else besides me? I have wrestled with it nearly all my life, and have landed on a conclusion, or perhaps part of one. My faith has gone through many changes over the years: from simple, child-like faith to intellectual agreement and on to my responsibility in using faith. From there, it kept growing from responsibility to duty. Up, up, up the faith ladder I climbed, until the day I reached the top and learned the particular ladder I depended on was leaning against the wrong wall. It got me absolutely nowhere. Well, that isn't altogether true, either. It landed me in the pit of despair. But thankfully it didn't end there. This time, searching for the truth about faith took me far beyond what I ever imagined, without leaving step number one: simple, child-like faith.

The Bible tells me that faith is substance and evidence. Really. When is the realization of what I hoped for going to knock on my door? I can't count the number of "faith messages" I have listened to over the years, the books I've read, or the people I've talked to, trying to see the same results I have heard so much about. The list is too long for me to go further. In any case, in my search for the true meaning of faith, I have touched on many aspects of it, all claiming to be the key that will unlock whatever is blocking the results I desired. Absolutely every one of them brought me back to step number one—child-like faith.

> Then Jesus called a little child to Him, set him in
> the midst of them, and said, "Assuredly, I say to you,
> unless you are converted and become as little children,
> you will by no means enter the kingdom of Heaven.
> Therefore whoever humbles himself as this little child
> is the greatest in the kingdom of Heaven. (Matthew
> 18:2–4; NKJV)

What is different about that simple kind of faith? Basically, children don't try. Give that statement a few moments of thought. Those few words may change everything.

CHILDREN DON'T TRY; THEY SIMPLY TRUST

A child doesn't think to determine the trustworthiness of the one they are placing their lives in. Their entire existence is simply given to someone else to take care of them. They give no second thought about it, without trying to figure it out. They have no worries about failure, and they don't work up trust. Children don't have to try.

Oh, boy! Is that ever an eye-opener for me. Working at faith had been an all-consuming concern in my life. It is always on the back burner of my thoughts, wondering if I had enough faith and how to get more if needed.

There was a time when the church was all about making very sure we were speaking words of faith. The right words at the right time was the equivalent of showing the right kind of faith. It didn't matter what the situation looked like, as long as I spoke my desired results correctly. If I failed in that point, my faith would come into question.

This was demonstrated on one of the worst nights of my life. My beloved dad, at age fifty-nine, suffered a heart attack. My husband took our children back to Grandpa and Grandma's house while my mother and I stayed at the hospital with Dad. I remember the last thing he said to me. He took my hand, squeezed it (I remember thinking how strong he was, even at that time), and told me his condition was very bad. Mom suggested I pray for him. All the thoughts about praying the correct words went through my mind. What if I spoke the wrong ones? What do I say? I knew Mom was counting on my prayer to make it all okay.

I don't even remember what I prayed, but I felt a sickness in my heart that I didn't do it right. I hugged him and kissed his cheek. Then Mom and I went home to change before we came back for the night. On our way home, her car broke down. It was very late at night, we were on a country road, and we had to walk back to the hospital, which took about an hour. Honest, this really happened. To most people, this would not be an issue, but dad was a master mechanic. Now, how many times does a master mechanic's car just stop running, late at night, in this kind of situation? I have the distinct feeling that we were kept away from the hospital by forces beyond our control. I don't even recall questioning that though, because my world was about to change forever, and questions like that would only serve to make things worse. Looking back, I can see that God was sheltering me from painful experiences and memories that would haunt me forever.

Upon our arrival at the hospital, we were greeted by a doctor who informed us that my dad was gone. The doctors and nurses worked on him for a long time but couldn't bring him back. Even after nearly thirty-eight years, I can still feel the dagger piercing my heart. The man who was my hero, my best friend growing up, the man who I believed to be the best father, ever, had died. My prayer had no effect on the situation whatsoever.

What should I have prayed? What words would have made the difference? The teaching that told me God would jump to the right words tormented me. I felt like I had caused my father's death.

It took a while, but the Holy Spirit sent me healing in regard to that night. One of the things He did was a great comfort to me. The story came back to us from the medical staff working on Dad, trying to bring him back. As they were working, someone in the room mentioned a strong, sweet aroma permeating the room. Looking around, there were no flowers or anything that could produce that sweet smell. This happened a couple more times; each time the sweetness got stronger. When Dad was gone, so was the aroma. I know what that was; it was the aroma of heaven filling the room. Heaven's citizens accompanied my precious father into eternity.

NO CONFIDENCE IN THE FLESH

I have come to the conclusion that word of faith teachings, as good as they are, are missing something vital. Missing this step made an amazing difference in my attitude, my view of the situation, my view of myself, and even the outcome of my prayer.

That ingredient is grace. People put all of their faith in their words instead of in God's grace. Confidence placed in knowledge, not solely on the work of the cross is powerless. The message I heard was, with the combination of the right words and enough faith; I always get what I want from God. One person stated it this way: this is how to write your own ticket with God.

Yes, I agree that much of the teaching about speaking the right words into situations is spot on. Yes, I agree that God has given us His authority on this earth to bring heaven's reality into circumstances we face. What happened to alter that message? What was missing for me was the cross. My trust is in the total success of the cross. Nothing else needs to be added, and to even think that I have a part in its success is an insult to that great redemptive act, and dare I say it, perhaps a little arrogant.

It takes humility to receive His grace. Reaching out to receive God's grace means letting go of my own efforts alone to obtain answers to prayer. I believe all good things flow from His great grace. It is the starting point from which every good thing emerges. Any other source either bends toward works or dives fully into them. Learn from Jesus. He did what He saw His Father do. When I follow His example and partner with the Holy Spirit by speaking His rhema words into situations, I am confident in His answer. I found that most of the time, waiting was another missing ingredient. Listen first for what God is saying about what you are praying for.

My husband and I have been involved in prayer ministry for years. We learned to wait for a few seconds before saying anything, even when the person you are praying for is standing before you. We proceed when we hear from the Holy Spirit. Usually I begin by praying what I sense the Holy Spirit is speaking into the situation. When I am finished, Darrell has always received a rhema word for the person, or a picture of how God sees the situation. It is always exactly what is needed, every time, without exception.

I have witnessed people coming into a praying situation with both guns loaded but with empty heads. They do not take the time to take aim. No time to see clearly, just shoot. It usually misses the target and hits all bystanders. Focused, yes, but often on the wrong target. Instead of waiting to see exactly what the target is, some prayers are more like shotguns instead of rifles.

What I saw happening in regard to praying for things wanted, was that people were putting their faith in *their words*, not in the favor and mercy of God. It almost felt as if I held the control over what I want in this world. And God, bless His heart, is obligated to fulfill my every request.

It was taught that, by speaking the right words, I can claim to produce the desired results. Please don't misunderstand me; I absolutely believe that God's words contain power to change situations and even the atmosphere we live in. I also completely believe that when we speak God's words, heaven's reality invades our situations. The difference is in where my faith is placed. I can partner with the Holy Spirit by praying as God sees things. That means that I pray with God, not to Him.

A prayer originates in heaven; I have no confidence in the flesh for answered prayer. I know many people whose lives were shipwrecked because of that one missing part of the message. They placed their confidence in what they said and how much faith went with their words. It can easily become a works-mentality dogma.

The heartbreaking consequence was that many threw away a great truth because it wasn't fully understood.

God resists the proud but gives grace to the humble. The truth is so amazing that some people completely missed it. God is delighted in His children and will give us our heart's desire when it is good for us. I already have everything stored for me in a place entitled: "everything needed to fulfill the Christian walk on the earth" (See Ephesians 1). Everything is mine already.

Where this took a detour is when faith was placed in my efforts, not in God's goodness.

DISAPPOINTMENTS

When disappointments move in, sometimes faith moves out or at least takes a hit. There are times when a disappointing situation is simply too difficult to ignore. Some crises require a little time out to find my way through the maze of emotional wreckage. Often, when I'm in the middle of a difficulty, I have one thing in my mind—I want out of this mess! God may want to take a little time, valuable time, time that it takes to know Him and His purposes.

Unfortunately, I had come to the mistaken conclusion that unhappy situations will never visit me, and if they did, it was because I had done something to cause it or missed doing something that was needed.

I have had my share of bitter disappointments. Those are times when all the usual answers out there only serve to create more pain. I know I'm not the only one who has faced a series of letdowns. Enough of them will just plain wear me out. Once in a while a crisis comes that threatens to plow my faith under to the point that I am afraid to trust again. Raging emotions, utter disappointment, unanswered questions tear at me like a deadly tornado, leaving my faith shattered and broken but not dead.

To deny those feelings is a mistake. They must be processed against God's word and in tandem with His character. Allow me to share a few helpful hints in dealing with deadly, faith-altering disillusionments. First, remember that emotions are neither good nor bad in value. They are simply feelings that need to be looked at and processed correctly. It's okay to say someone or something has let me down. My trust has been violated and has left me, bags packed, ready for the "home for the bewildered."

Second, know that it is okay to share every feeling, good or bad, with God. He already knows every thought and feeling, so it is impossible to surprise Him with details. If I am in a personal crisis, I try not to voice it to anyone else, and by all means, I don't put it on a prayer chain. If I really do need to talk to someone for support or counsel, I make sure it is someone who loves me without condition, no matter what, and that they carry—(this is important)—no condemnation or guilt. Most essential, I make sure they know how to keep their mouth shut. I am referring to needs of a very private nature. The majority of prayer needs should be shared. Corporate prayer is powerful. I'm just saying that it is important to be discerning about what is made public.

Third, ask the Lord what this situation is really about. So often, I discover that God sees things differently than I do. I see my answered prayer in a certain way; God may be after something entirely different. After I discover how He sees the situation, I will ask Him if there is something He wants me to do in this situation. I try to never ask why. It will only serve to give me more unanswered questions and lots of grief. I think I'll leave the "why" for heaven; then I'll ask away.

In reality, these kinds of problems are not about my disappointment. It is about walking through the disappointments without throwing away my faith. It is not about having or not having enough faith. It is not about working for God's favor. It is about me and my relationship with the Lord. My current situation tells me much about His love, His mercy, His purposes for me, and how to know what He is saying.

Before long, the tears are finished, the frustration has been released, and the anger has subsided. Now I can proceed without all the drama. During the storm, I tend to give credence to the emotions. Yes, they are real, but they may not contain the truth. I can't depend on them as truth when my soul is tormented by heartbreaking situations.

There are real issues here. Too many times I try to force my way through them with a courageous smile on my face, when all I want to do is go to bed and pull up the covers. It is at this point I have seen many people shipwrecked on the rocky shores during the storms of life.

Faith becomes much more than getting what I desire; it is seeing God's good desire for me. It is being seated with Christ is the heavenlies, where the view is much clearer. It is not claiming that I will never experience a storm. It is walking through storms because I know I am eternal; my purpose is eternal. Faith is when life becomes bigger than me.

FINDING A CONCLUSION

The only consistent thing in this life that anyone can count on is God's love. It never changes, diminishes, or turns away. There will be a day when I will trust again, without fear, because God will show me what things look like from His perspective.

That is when I see clearly. That is when faith is more than hope. It has substance. I move from hoping to seeing. The more I see *my* true identity and what God has done to bring me into union with Him, the more I know substance and evidence of things hoped for. It is the gospel. Signs and wonders follow, declaring the truth.

This is so simple that I just didn't get it. When dealing with complex things (like computers, for instance), I tell people that I need to get very basic, as in, where is the "on" button? My delightful granddaughter knows me well. When she teaches me something on the computer, she writes the procedure down, step-by-step, and which button to push next. So, please allow me to explain this in a way that makes sense to me. The subject matter is faith. It is not something to be striving for or working at. It is the exact opposite. It is something to let go. Let go of all the marvelous efforts to have more faith. Let go of the stress of having to measure up; I never really know how much is enough. Let go of the responsibility to achieve a standard that is God's alone.

Since every need I will ever have has already been accomplished by Jesus on the cross, it is wasted energy and time to try to work at having enough faith for it. Instead of thinking in those terms, think this way: it is finished already. Why work for something that is done? The cross is enough. Its purpose is fulfilled completely, and it is a total success. Don't keep your faith; let it go straight to the Father's heart. Let it go, and let the cross do the work. He knows it is already accomplished. I need to know it, too.

The next time I find myself in a problem situation, I need to ask myself this question: Does the Father have enough faith in what Jesus accomplished on the cross?

Faith is simply an effortless realization of the facts of Calvary. Does faith save you? No, Jesus saved you. Faith is recognizing the free gift God has already given. Ephesians 2:8 says, *"For it is by grace you have been saved, through faith—and this not from yourselves, it is a gift of God."*

What if God supplies us with everything needed for my salvation—even my faith? I hear preached everywhere that Jesus died to save you. The next thing I hear is, "Now it is up to you to believe in Jesus, confess your sins, get baptized, and then you will be saved." Most often a sinner's prayer follows this, just in case the person listening doesn't know what the right thing to do is. From then on, I hear one requirement after another to be saved and to stay saved.

Jesus died to save me. It happened long before I was born. That is the gospel. I have preached it successfully. Let the message do its work. Instead of adding human attempts to generate or maintain the experience, follow up with words of encouragement that endorse what just happened. A whole new horizon has come, full of promise and full of joy.

What if faith, from God's perspective, is recognizing what has already been accomplished by Jesus? Faith is putting my trust in Jesus' work, not in my ability to believe in Him. The great news is, I don't have to prove to God that I believe enough. That mindset only serves to create stress because I never know when I have reached enough faith. Religion has developed a strategy to cover bases by keep adding stuff to do and building up more faith for more stuff. It never ends.

Until I see that it's not about my strategic tactics or my calculated decision. It's not about me at all. It's about allowing the truth into my heart and mind that Jesus did it all. It is finished. Paul proclaimed to preach only one thing: Jesus Christ, crucified. It is enough. It is everything.

It is finished. Within that statement resides all evidences of the Christian walk. The facts are speaking loud and clear: I am a new creation. The old sin nature is dead and gone, and I don't give it another thought. When Jesus rose from the dead, my old nature did not. That is just the beginning. There are worlds of revelation held within that one act of redemption. The results are an endless wonder of God's love and purposes.

One after another, new truths are offered to me. I have the awesome privilege of partnering with the Holy Spirit as He reveals the full impact of the Godhead, as God is involved in my life.

I can make the choice to keep my thoughts aligned with what God says about me. I am a vessel that houses the Creator of all. I am a child of God, a joint-heir with Jesus. I am fully involved in the life of the Trinity. I am who God declares me to be. Faith is simply recognition of what Jesus has done. It is an effortless, joyful response that never ends because the discovery is so much bigger than I am.

How remarkable it is! God changed His address—to mine!

Faith is stepping into an already-existing reality. I am awakened to what Jesus has accomplished. This faith does not come with conditions. Faith is extreme in its simplicity; I make it difficult.

I know that faith will always be a hot topic of concern and discussion. The longer I am living, growing, and maturing in Christ, the more I realize its depth of simplicity. How can I say that faith is that simple? How can I say that such a complex subject is easy enough for a child? That's because it all occurred before you existed. Everything I put my faith in was a fact before I was. As a matter of fact, in God's mind, it was finished before the creation of the earth.

I live in the finished side of the cross. I put my trust in that fact. I was not involved in the process at all. It was complete long before I came along. So, my question is, why work on a finished project?

Before I leave this subject, there have been overwhelming conclusions about faith from scholars and theologians; about the faith of Jesus. Many verses speak about "faith in Jesus" when the actual translation should read "faith of Jesus."

> But now apart from the Law *the* righteousness of God has been manifested . . . even the righteousness of God which comes through the faith/faithfulness of Jesus Christ for all those who believe, for there is no distinction. (Romans 3:21–22)

> Romans 3:26 states—."for the demonstration, I say, of His righteousness at the present time, that He might be just and the justifier of the one who is of the faith of Jesus.'

> Galatians 2:16 says -"nevertheless knowing that a man is not justified by the works of the Law but through the faith of Christ Jesus, even we have believed in Christ Jesus, that we may be justified by the faith of Christ, and not by the works of the Law; since by the works of the Law shall no flesh be justified."

Galatians 2:20 states—"I have been crucified with
Christ; and it is no longer I who live, but Christ lives
in me, and the life which I now live in the flesh I live
by the faith/faithfulness of the Son of God, who loved
me, and delivered Himself up for me."

Galatians 3:22 states—"But the Scripture has shut up
all men under sin, that the promise by the faith of Jesus
Christ might be given to those who believe."

Ephesians 3:12 says-"in whom we have boldness and
confident access through His faith/faithfulness."

Philippians 3:9 reads—and be found in Him, not
having a righteousness of my own derived from the Law,
but that which is through the faith of Christ, the righteousness that comes from God on the basis of faith."

John Crowder said something very wonderful in his book Cosmos
Reborn: "The flavor of faith is not striving, contending or 'pressing in'
for something. The flavor of faith is rest. It is to trust in what someone
else has already accomplished for us."

So many people make faith the vehicle they use to obtain what
they desire. That means the results are entirely up to me; answers are
directly dependent on my faith-o-meter. My level of faith determines
God's answers.

God says faith is much simpler than that. It is placing the results in
the completed and thorough work of Jesus. So the question is not "Can
I generate enough faith?" but "What is Jesus' faith in this situation?" I
can trust in my efforts, or I can place my faith in what is already there
for me by Jesus. Everything visible has its origin in the invisible.

The Old Covenant is full of types and shadows of a future Savior.
Those people were sustained by hope. The cross is the place where hope
became substance, the unseen became evidence. Jesus is the shadow
the Old Testament prophets longed for. Jesus is the substance and the
answer to their hope. At the perfect time, what they hoped for became

reality. The promise was Jesus Christ. Now faith rests completely and totally in Him.

Jesus Christ has become our Sabbath Rest.

REST: THE OTHER SIDE OF THE COIN

The word *rest* will bring as many mental images as there are individuals. It occurs many times in the Bible. It means cessation, refreshment, to make to cease. Second Corinthians 12:9 talks of being covered by rest. Rest means "a tabernacle that is spread over me." It also means "to lodge or inhabit," and to "rest from labor." The Sabbath rest speaks of the rest of God Himself after creating the worlds, the universe, and all we see; even much we cannot see.

The word *rest* has many definitions and facets, each with countless ways God's rest affects our lives.

Personally, my rest is closely connected to my view of God, my identity, and my current situation in life. The reconciliation of all these things result in the degree of rest I actually experience.

There are hundreds of things trying to influence me every day. Most of them cause unrest, anxiety, or stress, and all want to dictate my thoughts, my emotions, and my choices. The degree of rest during these days is directly determined by how involved God is in the moments that make up my life. So many times, I encounter and proceed to take on stressful situations without even consulting the Lord or what He thinks about it. All the intelligent figuring in the world cannot replace including God in the equation.

Too often, I have found myself taking a detour, only to discover a mile or two down the road that it was a mistake. I tell myself that I knew better than to go that direction! So, I put the whole process in reverse and start over.

I have great news! The day of regret is over. There is no longer a reason to beat myself up over poor choices—no more fighting for resolution before I see some respite and no more scheming and conniving to achieve some relief. Something wonderful is available. It is called rest.

Our God is very personal. He speaks my language, giving me words and insight that tell me that He knows. He knows everything. He knows my thoughts before I do and fully anticipates the blessings He plans to pour out on me.

Exodus 3 tells an amazing story of a man who discovered God in a most unusual way. A bush was on fire but was not consumed. Who would think of such a thing? A creative genius, that's who! It certainly got Moses' attention. Then the bush began a conversation with him.

Moses asked God who He was. He certainly was someone who did not run in the same social circles as he was used to. Did He have a name? Remember, names were very meaningful in those days. In those days a person's name described them and often their destiny. What was the name of this One in the burning bush? I AM THAT I AM. Okay. Can you be a little more specific? I AM means Yahweh or Jehovah. It describes God's unchangeable power and character. Moses was raised in Pharaoh's house, where several different gods were worshipped. He may not have realized the meaning of the name given him by the bush, but I am quite sure his fellow Israelites did. I AM reminded them of their Father Abraham and the promise of their own land. It was that very covenant that God would fulfill through Moses.

I AM. I am what? I am who? Basically, I AM whatever and whoever you need Me to be today. Right now. Do you need something in your life today? I AM what you need. I AM your peace. I AM your provision. I AM your wisdom. I AM your strength. I AM absolutely everything you will ever need. I AM the completion of the covenant. I AM your rest.

Centuries later, Jesus makes His appearance. He was I AM in a human body. I think Rest must have been His middle name. He slept through a violent storm at sea, like a baby being rocked by his devoted mother. When awakened by the terror of His shipmates, Jesus tells the winds and waves to chill out. He is Rest personified.

To those who are weary and burdened-down, those who don't know which way to turn, and those who are worn out by life, Jesus offers great hope. It is called rest. He says to take on His yoke because it is easy.

A yoke is the harness that tethers two oxen together, so they can share the load and maneuver heavy objects. Taking on Jesus' yoke may mean to let Him carry the burden of sin, or religious requirements and commands, and of life in general. Okay. That sounds wonderful, but it still leaves a question in my mind. A yoke of oxen requires two animals, which implies teamwork—sharing the load. That is a little problematic for me, especially when I came to believe that He carried all my sin with Him to the cross and buried it with Him in the grave. However, when Jesus rose from His tomb, my sin did not! At that moment my sin was exchanged for His righteousness. I had no part in the process of redemption.

A few years ago I came across another possible interpretation of the subject of yokes. They are both good, but this one sounds more like the gospel. In the culture of Jesus' day, a rabbi was the authority in interpretation of Scripture. These men devoted their entire lives to learning and sharing their belief in what God's Word said. They were the religious experts in understanding the Holy Scriptures.

If you found a rabbi whose teaching you could relate to, and under whom you could learn Scripture, you would sit under his teaching, much like finding a church today. When you found the rabbi of your choice to learn from, you were "taking on his yoke."

The religious spirit of that day was, well, very religious. People were carrying heavy burdens of behavior and rules to follow if they were to honor God—until Rabbi Yeshua began to teach. His teaching in the marketplaces and hillsides was different. He is quoted in Matt. 11:28-30 as telling people to *"Come to Me, all you who labor and are heavy laden, and I will give you rest. Take My yoke upon you and learn from Me, for I am gentle and lowly in heart, and you will find rest for your souls. For My yoke is easy and My burden is light."* Jesus yoke is easy and light. You feel rest in your soul. I believe Jesus is saying, "I don't want to help you with your burden, I want to carry it for you and give you My righteousness, whereby you will honor the Father."

First Peter 5:7 says to *"cast all your care on Him, for He cares for you."* The example has been given of a packhorse that carries the load. The person lets go of the burden, casts it on the horse, and lets the horse carry it. Cast your burden on Jesus, and let Him do the caring for you.

Rest. That's where I want to live.

REST—IN GOD'S DICTIONARY

The book of Hebrews has a great deal to say about the subject of rest. Chapter 3 describes what happened when the children of Israel entered a time period that God referred to as "the rebellion."

How does God describe rebellion? In one word, it is unbelief. Most people will think of rebellion in terms of wrong choices or being unwilling to walk the line. Some think rebellion is about falling short of fulfilling the conditions and requirements of the Law. One would think so. Religion tells us that is truth. God's description of rebellion is different. Do you ever wonder why?

I would like to take a look at a very momentous day in history. The day that a four hundred year promise was about to be fulfilled. Remember God's promise to Abraham? He was going to be the father of many nations, with countless descendants. They would settle in a land promised just for them—a perfect land with everything they would need to thrive. That promise was told and retold throughout generations. "The promise" kept the people as they endured bondage and slavery. It was something solid to hang on to when things were at their worst. Someday it will be reality. The entire account is in Numbers, chapters one through twenty-two.

Finally, after a series of very dramatic supernatural events, that day came! The day! The day—the promise—made centuries ago, was about to be reality. All the dreams, all the hopes and prayers, and all the tears and years of waiting came to *this day*.

Can you imagine how the people felt? The excitement must have been so real they could almost see it. Some people were feeling a little nervous, and not as sure as others that this is the right day or maybe the right place. Perhaps they should go in and see for themselves first. After all, no one has gone in there before, and it is better to be prepared. So went their reasoning.

What was right in front of their eyes? The promise made to them by God himself! Of course, it was perfect. Don't you remember the promises, the stories, and the prophecies? It looked like they not only forgot what God had promised, they also forgot their centuries in bondage. They forgot their miraculous deliverance from Egypt. They forgot their elation at seeing their enemies' dead, never to come after them again. After 400 years of constantly looking behind them to see if their mortal enemy is after their head, God showed them a memory that would erase that fear forever.

Read what happened. They selected a "committee" to check out the new land, just to be sure. The twelve men were selected as spies to see for themselves. They looked around at everything. Yes, it was perfect! Everything they could ever dream of was there. There was, however, one obstacle—giants—big ones. They were so big that ten of the spies compared themselves as grasshoppers next to them. You will find this account in Numbers, chapter fourteen.

Two of the twelve spies came back, beside themselves with excitement. They saw everything that the other ten saw. They saw the giants, too, but they did not compare themselves to them; they compared the giants to their God. There was no contest. I can imagine them saying, "We can take them. We will eat them for breakfast; they are our bread! Listen to us, brothers, the giants are *toast!*"

Caleb is described as a man with a different spirit. While ten men came back with the mentality of a grasshopper, Caleb came back as a giant killer! He knew it, his countrymen knew it, and his enemy knew it!

What a difference an outlook makes. Ten men looked at the obstacle, but two looked at the possibilities. Ten were overcome with fear and with doubt. Two were convinced in God's ability to perform miracles. Ten men were influenced by a lie; not one trusted in the promise as much as about their own faulty identity. Their perception of themselves fell far short of God's opinion. Two men believed that their God was more than an object to be worshipped; He was personal and intimate. His relationship with His people went far beyond rules and regulations to follow. They believed that their God cared about them and their lives.

I'm sorry to say the two believing men, Joshua and Caleb, were drowned out by the fear the others placed on the people. Theirs were voices that did not even bring God into their conclusions. They forgot who God was. They forgot who they were.

What did God call that scenario? He called it "the rebellion." Because of their mindset, only two men of that generation made it into the Promised Land. The rest of the people did not see the promise that was theirs to possess.

But take note: their children and their grandchildren did! God does not forget His promises! Even during the forty-year detour in the desert, God was still there for them. Even while dealing with their heart of unbelief, God's heart of mercy prevailed. Absolutely everything they could need was provided for them. He gave them manna when they were hungry. I have often wondered what manna tasted like. It sounds yummy, but they tired of it—manna al dente, manna burgers, sautéed manna, manna soufflé, even *bamanna bread*!

"Thank you very much, God, but we need meat."

"Okay, you want meat? Watch for it—mountains of quail."

Now they could prepare quail and manna stew.

They got thirsty. "This is the desert, for crying out loud! Would have been better to stay slaves, chomping on leeks and garlic than to die of thirst in the desert."

"Fine. You want water? I have a special source prepared for just this occasion. The water is in the rock. It will follow you through the desert."

The Apostle Paul mentions that miracle in the desert in his second letter to Corinth, chapter 10. The Rock that provided water in the desert was none other than Jesus Himself who offered living water—water that would quench thirst forever.

This rebellious, unbelieving generation did not experience the promise, but they still experienced God's heart of mercy without conditions or stipulations. God simply showed up and took care of every need, even when they were full of unbelief and complaints. No doubt about it, these were difficult people who always saw the negative and refused to believe God would fulfill His promise. They complained constantly about how they were mistreated. If that sounds vaguely familiar, take inventory of your mindset, your attitudes, your words, and what you believe. Your Promised Land is waiting for you.

THE PARTY'S ON!

Rest. God's promise is still in effect today. Hebrews, chapters three and four, tells us that the promise remains—the promise of rest.

> Therefore, do not be calloused in heart as the people of Israel were: every time they faced any contradiction in the wilderness, their response immediately revealed irritation rather than their faith. (Hebrews 3:8)

> Faith realized our entrance into God's rest. Hear the echo of God's cry through the ages, "Oh! If only they would enter into My rest." His rest celebrates perfection.

His work is complete; the fall of humanity did not flaw its perfection. (Hebrews 4:3)

It is clear then that there is still an opportunity to enter into that rest which Israel failed to access because of their unbelief, even though they were the first to hear the good news of God's intention to restore mankind to the same Sabbath that Adam and Israel had lost. (Hebrews 4:6)

The conclusion is clear: the original rest is still in place for God's people. (Hebrews 4:9)

Rest can mean many things. The reference in Hebrews is referring to God's rest. What exactly does that mean? Let's go all the way back to the beginning. It took God six days to create the world and everything in it—the universe and so much I can't even begin to fathom. When day seven came, God looked around. It was good. It was perfect. It was finished. So, what did He do? He rested and enjoyed His completed creation.

This rest has nothing to do with feeling weary. It has everything to do with celebration. When people consider creation, all they see is lots of work. Not so with God. He spoke. The power in His words literally created something out of nothing. I truly believe He was beside Himself with joy as He spoke the universe into existence. From the expanse of the universe to the smallest creature, all creation gave Him great joy. The spoken, uttered words of God literally create.

Science today has discovered that sound keeps traveling. There is no stopping point. Imagine speaking God's truth into the atmosphere over your home, your family, your sphere of influence. His Words are still powerfully creative today.

Several years ago we were with friends on July 4. The fireworks were just out of sight down the river, but we could see the blast of light and hear the explosion. As I was sitting there watching this, I saw the flash of light first, and then, two seconds later, I heard the blast. The Holy Spirit kept telling me to pay attention to the sound. As I was listening, I saw in my imagination the sound waves bouncing off the mountains that lined the river. They were full of power. It was as if anything in its way was sent tumbling away at the impact of the sound. The force of the sound was so mighty that nothing could stand in its way. The Holy Spirit was showing me what God's words look like from His perspective. They are not merely words, but strength and power, send out to accomplish His intentions.

Words carry energy, both negative and positive. As I partner with God, as He desires to invade the earth with heaven's realities, I can speak His words that change the atmosphere. Praise and worship are power words that bring God's presence. Negativity is the worship of hell, which, when spoken can cause discouragement and defeat.

SABBATH REST

Creation was complete; every detail, perfect. It was finished. God took the time to rest and enjoy what He created. That is called a Sabbath rest, or a rest from working. Hebrews 4:9–10 encourages us to enter into God's rest. "There remains, therefore, a rest for the people of God. For he who has entered his rest has himself ceased from his works, as God did from His." By entering into God's rest, into Sabbath rest, we enter into a completed work. We enter into what Jesus meant when, just before death, He said, "It is finished" (John 19:30).

Andrew Murray, a 19th- century author, said:

> We do not always enjoy the blessings and power of Jesus' blood because we don't always understand what it means or don't actively co-operate with it in our lives. God has provided that Jesus' blood still has power and carries on its work in us today. *My weakness cannot interfere with the power of the blood.* The blood continues its active work-no matter what! I submit myself to the sanctifying power of Jesus' blood. That's all I do. Can we trust completely in His accomplishment? (emphasis mine)

When I enter into Jesus' finished work, I let go of my effort to gain righteousness. It is the difference between works *for* righteousness (my effort to become righteous), and works *of* righteousness (the righteousness of God working in and through my life).

> He takes away the first (Old Covenant) that He may establish the second (New Covenant). By that will *we have been sanctified* through the offering of the body of Jesus *once for all* (emphasis mine) ... Now where there is remission of these (sin), there is no longer an offering for sin. (Hebrews 10:10, 18)

Let me tell you, friends, this is good news!

Often people have problems when they try to figure this out. My suggestion is—don't even go there. It is not comprehendible from the place of human logic. When I ask for Divine revelation, I am able to see from God's viewpoint.

I came face-to-face with decades of traditions and religious thought, held them up to the light of God's grace, and made a decision. It caused some tension, but that is good. It means something is happening. It means I am forced to take a good look at what I believe and why I believe it. My personal conclusion gave me something no one can argue with.

I must confess I did my share of arguing with the Lord about this. What about when I miss the mark and make a mistake? What about sin? I have a couple of answers for those questions. First, yes, there are times when I miss the target I am aiming at or don't even aim at all. I judged myself harshly, then often turned the judgment onto others.

I discovered a couple of scriptures that completely answer those questions.

> Jesus is our at-one-ment, He has conciliated us to Himself and has taken our sins and distortions out of the equation. What He has accomplished is not to be seen as something that belongs to us exclusively; the same at-one-ment includes the entire kosmos! (1 John 2:2; MIRROR)

> But also for this very reason, giving all diligence, add to your faith virtue, to virtue knowledge, to knowledge

self-control, to self-control perseverance, to perseverance godliness, to godliness brotherly kindness, and to
brotherly kindness love. For if these things are yours
and abound, you will be neither barren nor unfruitful
in the knowledge of our Lord Jesus Christ. For he who
lacks these things is shortsighted even to blindness, and
has forgotten that he was cleansed from his old sins. (2
Peter 1:5–9; NKJV)

I vividly remember being alarmed at the growing evil surrounding us.
Someone once said that if God does not judge the United States (and
most all nations) for the evil in them, He would have to apologize to
Sodom and Gomorrah. It is crucial to remember that Jesus was judged
for all mankind: past, present, and future. If God were to judge during
this age of grace, He would have to apologize to Jesus! The same is true
when I judge others.

It is actually very easy. That's what makes it so hard for some. So
here I am at point A, hearing new thoughts, struggling with my "stuff."
I want to grow out of here and enter into rest. I want to abide in rest. I
want to live there, think there, and breathe in that rest. What do I have
to do? How does this happen?

What if I were to say, *I am already there*! It happened at Calvary, by
Jesus, on my behalf. It is finished! It is absolutely, unconditionally, completely, utterly, totally *for me*!

Quoting Graham Cooke's Game Changer series: "When God looks
at you, He doesn't see anything wrong with you. You are perfect because
of the blood of His Son. He sees what is missing in your experience with
Him, and He can't wait to give you those things."

THERE IS ONE

There is one who is consumed with my sin. He does not want me to
know the truth of the gospel. He does not want me to rest in Jesus' work.
Sin is very important to him. Why? Because if he can cause believers to
focus on sin in their life, he has a foothold into their destruction. The
first step in his strategy is to find a hook somewhere and infiltrate any
area where Jesus isn't in control. We all know his name: Satan. I have

good news, however; He cannot touch us without finding a place to hook us—no hook, no influence.

Do I need to guard my heart? Yes I do, but not because of God's judgment or wrath. I stay hidden in Christ because of our enemy. Are my choices important? Of course they are, not because God will be angry, but because fear involves judgment, torment, and punishment— the very things Jesus has taken for me, and from me.

Rest is so much more than I realize. When we live in this rest, my enemy has no access to me. There is no foothold for him to grasp.

Rest becomes a weapon. I am resting, not in my works, but in the finished work of Jesus Christ. That puts the cross between me and anything our enemy can throw at me.

I am in Christ.

I know my identity, and my purpose.

I am dangerous to the darkness.

The reality is, Satan is not my enemy; *I am his enemy*!

Rest is a weapon!

A QUESTION FOR YOU

Faith and rest are two sides of the same coin.

What would happen if you simply let go of all your efforts and put that effort into simply believing in the finished work of Jesus? What changes could you see happening in your life if you were to embrace the gospel in all of its truth? Can you accept that? Can you abandon yourself to His grace?

We are all on a journey. Each person at a different place, all good.

Learn to love the learning. Even if we have difficulty letting go of some old stuff; even if we argue with the Lord from time to time, He is not troubled with our questions. As a matter of fact, I think He enjoys them.

The answers are always an adventure in joyful discovery.

CHAPTER 9

HIGH DEFINITION

SEEING WITH GRACE-COLORED GLASSES

When the truth of God's amazing grace goes deep into my heart and mind, life will never be the same. Be ready to live life in a new normal, from a new perspective, with a new mindset and language. This new normal means living heaven to earth. I am human, and I carry heaven's reality everywhere I go.

For those sci-fi groupies out there, I can honestly say that I am a human host for an extra-terrestrial life form! His name is Holy Spirit, and what adventure He brings to my life!

High definition, crystal clear thinking, and virtual reality are some words that define our society today. Technology has reached the point where new inventions outdate themselves on an almost daily basis. I am inundated with gadgets that can take me around the globe. I can have any information about anything within a few seconds, all packaged in something that can fit easily in my hand.

I firmly believe that God is doing the same things on a spiritual level in His church. Things that have been mysteries for centuries are becoming clear. There is a new wind blowing that causes us to see things in a new light. It is blowing away mindsets and belief systems that bind people to lifeless duty and obligations that have nothing to do with faith. New understanding of the Word is leaping off the pages and into hearts and minds all over the world, all at the same time, and without contact with each other. The Holy Spirit is orchestrating everywhere the same truths, even using the same words through total strangers. This has happened to me many times, and it never ceases to amaze me.

Often, when in study or thought, I hear something new from the Holy Spirit, something I had not known or considered before. Within hours or days, I see the exact same words written by someone I have never heard of and do not know. The world of technology has nothing over Holy Spirit communication. He is bringing a new way of thinking, maybe even to the point of changing and bringing insight into what I believe.

God is up to something big. I can feel it.

At the same time, I see the darkness getting deeper. People with limited insight will see only the darkness and can easily be overcome with fear. That is why I have purposed to share the powerful truth of the gospel. To those with the gift of evangelism who are reading this right now, I applaud you. Your voice is desperately needed in these times. As much as I would like it to be, evangelism is not my gift. I am a teacher and an encourager. My focus is intent on teaching the believing church the truth of who God really is and who He has created us to be in these days.

Like Lazarus of old, whom Jesus raised to life after being in the tomb for four days, many people are living, breathing believers but are still bound in their old grave clothes. Yes, they truly believe. Yes, they are saved and heaven-bound. My questions would be: Are they living the life God has for them, and are they bringing heaven's reality to the earth's situations? I see many wonderful people today who fear going beyond the religious fence that has kept them from fulfilling their true destiny. They are still confined in their old, dead, religious garments.

This message about grace and freedom is wonderful for the individual, but it cannot stop there. Imagine if believers everywhere caught God's vision for empowerment in their lives. What will happen when the church rises to her potential in the power of the Holy Spirit? It is called *revolution,* and we are in the beginning of one. Our faith, our vision, our hearts, everything we believe, is being revolutionized and energized to prepare us for this global mission. That is when my faith becomes far bigger than I am. God's truth breaks out of my life and into the world around me.

And that is the whole point from the beginning. The truth was not meant to stay inside church doors. Believers don't go to church; they are the church. The church goes out into the neighborhoods, shops, workplaces, schools; every place their feet touch becomes potential for Kingdom reality.

This chapter is not about, what is in it for me? On the other hand it is all about, what is in it for me. There is nothing more thrilling than to see God touch lives because you listened to His voice and followed His lead. This chapter is about seeing the world in high definition; from heaven's view.

Jesus was amazing at this. When He would come into a situation that had a specific need (which was constantly), He listened for heaven's take on the problem and then followed through with that direction. And He means for us to do exactly the same thing today. We have limited vision and insight; God sees beyond the surface, straight into the heart of the matter, and gives encouragement, healing, comfort, and edification. Biased thoughts, our own brokenness, and many other things can influence our judgment and often taint our limited conclusions.

God has one motive, one conclusion, and one objective: redemption and restoration, the result of His unconditional love. He is all about healing the brokenhearted, and He knows exactly where every heart is broken and how it needs to be healed. All I do is to listen to the Holy Spirit's voice, make it a purpose to lay aside all preconceived ideas or conclusions, and proceed under HSP (Holy Spirit Perception). I am a vessel. Period. And what an honor that is; to be an instrument of blessing in God's hands. That fact alone is mind-bending.

With that in mind, allow me to share some practical ways to live heaven to earth.

CHECKING MY ATTITUDE

I see something today that saddens me greatly. Actually, this has been in existence as long as I can remember. It is the attitude Christians have toward those who aren't living up to their standards or, using their own words, the "*sinners.*" It has bothered me for a long time that believers show no respect for nonbelievers. There is an air of self-righteousness that is so prevalent; it is no wonder why people don't want to listen to what Christians say.

So often I hear and feel very non-Christlike attitudes and words coming from those who claim to know Jesus. I see a great deal of anger toward those who have chosen another way. Of course that is always accompanied by accusations, making sure those listening know how very sinful they are. Shame, guilt, and condemnation are the tactics these people who believe with all their hearts that they are preaching the gospel. That is not the gospel.

The first argument I hear about this point is that Jesus severely preached about sin. No, He didn't—not in the way we think He did, anyway. Jesus lived and taught the Law even stronger than the Pharisees and teachers of the day. Jesus taught God's righteous standards. He told people what God's perception of righteousness was. And, of course, it was far beyond human ability to achieve; even the best of the best fall short of perfection.

What was Jesus doing? He was preparing the people to see their need for a Savior. Yes, He taught God's truth, but God's truth is impossible to achieve by human standard and effort. And, friends, that is the purpose of the New Covenant; to show us God's righteousness and provide the way to it.

> For God so loved the world that He gave His only begotten Son, that whosoever believes in Him shall not perish, but have everlasting life. For God did not send His Son into the world to condemn the world, but that the world through Him might be saved. (John 3:16–17)

THE MESSAGE

My first question to our "Bible-thumping" friends is about the message being preached. There are many voices out there, all wanting to be heard, and all saying that they have the only truth. We need the insight from heaven to see through the fog and discern truth from fiction. I see the need to slice through the dogma that runs on fear, stresses behavior control, and creates fences instead of bridges.

So, which will it be? Telling people about their sin and condemning them, or telling them about a God who loves them without strings attached, without conditions or requirements?

First, preaching behavior modification does absolutely nothing to change men's hearts. All that accomplishes is to alienate and anger people. It gives a false impression of who God really is. For decades all I knew God to be was judge, jury, and executioner unless, of course, I obeyed every commandment and fulfilled every requirement set before me. Even then it wasn't a sure thing because I was completely worthless and underserving of anything good. At least that is what I heard. God was good, of course, if and when all the conditions were right.

The messages I hear today are similar to those I grew up with. Judgment is at the core of these messages. What I did not realize is that God already made judgment when Jesus took my place on the cross. A divine exchange happened on Calvary. He who know no sin embraced my sinfulness. He took my sorrow, my pain, and my shame to His grave and exchanged that for His righteousness. He took my sin; I became His innocence. That is the truth of the gospel in its simplest definition. Of course, there is so much more in that act of love that it may well take eternity to discover.

Love is at the heart of the gospel, not judgment, guilt, shame, or condemnation, but unconditional love. This love knows no limits or boundaries; even my shortcomings cannot dilute it. That is the message that needs to be shouted from every corner. And in order for that to happen, the messengers need to understand it, and receive it for themselves. I cannot give what I have not received.

I know some folks who have decided they have the right to judge those outside of their religious persuasion. Before I go down that road, I need to understand that there is only one judge, and it is not me. Judgment was already finished for the entire human race many centuries ago at Calvary. It is over. Paul gives some insight in 1 Corinthians, which states:

> Any judgment prior to the Lord's coming (prior to the cross) is out of context. (The days of performance-based judgment are over!) His coming illuminates all the hidden mysteries (concerning man's inclusion in the death and resurrection of Christ.) and unveils the deepest desire of the heart of man. In His appearing (through the proclamation of this gospel) shall every man be commended by God. (1 Corinthians 4:5; Mirror Bible)

The love of Christ resonated within us and leaves us with only one conclusion: Jesus died humanity's death; therefore, in God's logic every individual simultaneously died. (1 Corinthians. 5:1)

And He Himself is the propitiation for our sins, and not for ours only but also for the whole world. (1 John 2:2)

Can you see it? That is the message the world is longing to hear. That is the gospel.

TSUNAMI!

About ten years ago I heard the Lord's voice very distinctly. It was so clear that I wrote it down, word for word. This is what He told me:

Like a giant tsunami, I am sending a new wave of My Spirit on the earth. It will begin on the coastland and continue inland. This will be a new thing; a new understanding. Lay aside all of your methods, all of the things you are used to doing, all of your old mindsets, because this will be new. It is about kingdom.

I must confess that at the time I was clueless to what the message meant. I understood tsunamis, and I understood what it meant to lay down old stuff. That was the extent of my understanding. Since then, however, it has become very clear to me. Today I see it happening where I live—in my church and in people I know. Not only that, but I see it happening throughout the nations as well.

I live on the Pacific Coast. Not long ago, we got word of some people on the East Coast who received the exact same message. The Holy Spirit connected us, and they have traveled to our region to pray in the tsunami of God's kingdom. They have prepared the way, and the waves are beginning to roll in. Something wonderful about this wave is that it is a wave of grace. That is the message of God's kingdom.

As we have seen, tsunamis are not selective about what they touch or cover. That tells me that no one is safe from His grace; no one is safe from a blessing. Those who believe and those who don't are both are being affected by God's amazing grace. His Kingdom is being established everywhere; some people are fully aware and engaged in it, and others will get the glory fallout just by being near.

THE REVOLUTION HAS BEGUN

We are in the beginning of a spiritual revolution. It is God's doing completely. Let me give you some definitions of a revolution:

- An overthrow of government (religious)
- A foundational change in power.
- A complete change in constitution.
- A movement which replaces one government with one based on a substantially different principle.
- Far-reaching changes in ways of thinking and acting.
- Fundamental change in value.
- Transformation.
- A procedure back to its starting point.

Every one of those definitions are absolutely accurate to what I am seeing happening in our world today. It is literally bringing God's kingdom reality into lives. The transformation is phenomenal. People are no longer living for God; God is living His life through us—*for others*. Now that is revolutionary!

LIVING LIFE ON PURPOSE

I am definitely a purpose-driven individual. I am happiest when I am in project with a purpose. My purpose is to live in high-definition. My purpose is to see what God sees, hear His voice, and follow His direction. My greatest desire is to make a difference in this world, at the very least, to the people who know me.

There have been a few times when this has been a remarkable reality to me. I will change the name here to protect someone I care about deeply. Let's call her Miss C.

I was invited to help with a theater project, designing and painting sets for an upcoming production. The team leader is a good friend of mine. She told me about Miss C., who was eager to learn to paint and asked if I would work with her. Of course! I would be delighted to do that!

In a short time I noticed someone backstage that I did not know, who was about six feet tall, wearing bib overalls, with a butch haircut, I believed that this person was a female but wasn't positive. She went to great lengths to appear otherwise. Within moments I was introduced to Miss C. Okay, now I have a new acquaintance. Another few minutes informed me that Miss C. has chosen to live an alternative lifestyle. That also answered a question or two. We went to work, painting, teaching some brush techniques and shortcuts, and how to get the effect you want from the audience's view.

As it turned out, I was the oldest person on the team, and everyone there decided to "mother" me, making sure I did not take any chances on a ladder or do anything unsafe. Unsafe to them and unsafe to me are two different things! I knew I had some back issues and soon discovered that Miss C. did, too.

As we were working on one set, she was literally on the ground, painting the bottom of the scene. I argued with her that I should be down there, being probably a foot shorter and closer to the ground. The words that she spoke are still speaking to my heart today. She said, "I would rather take the pain than to see you hurt."

It seemed like the world stopped for a moment. The Holy Spirit began downloading into my heart and mind the fact that when God created Miss C., He put His very heart of mercy in her. He also instructed me to give her that message. He concluded by telling me not to call anything unclean that He has made clean.

Wow. I thought about that brief encounter all evening. It addressed many things that I, as a Christian, needed to take a careful look at through the eyes of the Father. I did write it all out on a card and gave it to her the next day, letting her know what a profound effect she had on me. After hugs, tears, and more hugs, we finished our project, and began a friendship. She is a beautiful child of God, made in His image. I am extremely honored to be a part of her life.

PERCEPTIONS

We are all on a journey. As we grow in the stature of Jesus, the process involves changing the way we see, think, and even act. I believe there are many things God wants Christians to know about Christianity.

As He teaches me, I will experience major changes in myself and my perceptions of the truth, in the way I relate to others, and perhaps even in what I believe to be truth. Truth is based on God's Word. I believe this to be true. I also believe that in these days the Holy Spirit is opening up God's Word to reveal truth beyond what we have ever seen before.

Jesus came from heaven to teach us the truth about His kingdom. He came to show us heaven's mindset, how heaven thinks. He taught us the language of heaven, what heaven says. And He showed us how to be a citizen of heaven and of earth at the same time.

Here is a novel idea. Having been in pastoral ministry for decades, I believe I can say this with clarity and truth. I believe pastors would do very well to stick to two subjects; who God is (that can take an eternity) and who we are in Christ (we have only just begun.) If pastors will do that, something amazing will happen. The people under his care will begin to know the Holy Spirit intimately, recognize His voice, and hear from Him on a consistent basis. The pastor will have a church full of purpose, destiny, and people who are fulfilled in their lives. Their church will be examples of what it looks like to live heaven to earth; bringing heaven's realities into earth's situations.

APPLE SEEDS

A long time ago, I learned a wonderful lesson about fruit. While peeling an apple, I heard the voice of the Holy Spirit speak—"The issue is, not how many seeds are in the apple, but how many apples are in the seed. Where is your perspective?" Of course, I can count how many seeds are in an apple; it ranges from about six to twelve, depending on the kind of apple. But the apples that are contained in one seed cannot be counted. Millions upon millions over the centuries; one seed can produce itself over and over for generations.

Is that not the church's goal? Let's begin by giving the seed every-thing it needs to reproduce and then letting its Creator do His work in their lives.

INFLUENCES

When I begin to try to influence someone, it usually does not work at all. God does not want us to do stuff to win people to the Lord. He wants to simply let Him live His life through us.

I remember distinctly one evening at a meeting where people were singing a song that literally begged God to come down. There were many tears and lots of anguish. As I was standing there, I realized that I just could not join in this ritual. I had no doubt that it was sincere and honest, but something in me felt that it just wasn't the truth. After an SOS to heaven, I got an answer. It began small but became louder by the second. The voice was the Holy Spirit. His message: "Let me out! Let me out!"

It is not about me; it is about who I carry.

So many believers today are very fearful of the world. I don't under-stand that. Don't they realize that the world has no influence over us? It is actually the other way around. And it isn't by any means that I can conjure up; it is by the Holy Spirit living through me.

I was given a most amazing compliment one day, many years ago. I was moving to another city, and the place I worked wanted to give me a going-away party. I was so honored, and thrilled. One person in partic-ular said something publically that I will never forget. She said that she had known many Christians in her life, but only one who really lived it. That one was me. I am not bragging, except on my Lord Jesus Christ who lives in me and loves through me. I am undone.

SPECIAL ASSIGNMENT: COMIC RELIEF

During our years pastoring, we would always have a holiday event, or play, or something special to remember the day. One Easter will for-ever burn in my memory as the funniest thing I have ever seen. Please let me set the stage—literally.

The church had high ceilings, a raised platform, and a built-in baptis-tery along the back wall of the platform. On either side of the baptistery were steps going down to a small dressing room, one for gentlemen and one for ladies. When not in use, the baptistery was covered by a heavy drape.

The play was about Jesus' resurrection and ascension. In my imagination I could see Jesus ascending in a cloud of fog, from a heavy wood platform that covered the baptistery. When it was obvious to the audience that he was going up, the drapes would be drawn and the effect would be perfect.

Armed with my idea, I went to the men of the cast to help me out with the details. My husband, a very clever man, suggested using a heavy plank where Jesus would stand on one end, and the other end would be used, like a teeter-totter down the stairs, thus lifting our Jesus off the ground for the two seconds necessary. The drapes would close at the end of the scene.

The other men in the cast, however, were very industrious with their idea. They devised a harness that Jesus would wear, which was attached to a rope, which was attached to a pulley, which was attached to the point in the ceiling directly twenty feet above Jesus.

Then came the dress rehearsal. Any person ever associated with the theater understands that if anything goes wrong, that will be the night. We kept up that tradition, plus added indescribable hilarity.

I was watching the whole scene from a chair on the platform. Jesus was secured in his harness, so far so good. A couple of Herculean men began to pull on the rope. The first thing that set me over the edge into uncontrollable laughter was the squeak in the pulley. I was full of apology, but I just couldn't help myself.

As Jesus was being pulled up, his shoulders moved. Nothing else did. When his shoulders were about ear level, his toes barely touching the ground, his arms hanging in a grotesque, rag doll sort of way, I noticed a look of terror begin to creep into his eyes. As soon as he lifted up from solid ground he began slowly spinning, much like a roasted animal on a vertical pit.

By that time, I couldn't even sit up, I was laughing so hard. Laying on the floor, trying to look sympathetic, but totally overcome with hysterics, we decided to go with the teeter-totter. It worked perfectly.

If you can't see God with a sense of humor, I am truly sorry. I know He was laughing along with the rest of us, except maybe for the man that portrayed Jesus. I think he just wanted out of the harness.

SPIRITUAL WARFARE

The church these days is awakened to darkness around us. No doubt, the darkness is growing, and seems like it is looking directly into our eyes, daring us to do something about it. There are many powerful prayer groups arising, preparing the battleground for war. It is real, and many people are in grave danger.

The most important issue in this battle is determining who the enemy is. There is only one real enemy, and he is after the demise of God's kingdom. He has already lost the battle and the war, but he is so full of hate that he will not be satisfied until he has caused as much damage as possible.

There are warriors all around us. People are praying, the hosts of heaven who are armed and dangerous, and perhaps the most dangerous of all are unassuming, normal people who go about their ordinary days seemingly oblivious to the warfare around them but are indeed fully aware and armed with weapons that cannot be conquered.

The first weapon everyone considers is, of course, prayer. That is absolutely true. We all need to be listening for our commander's voice for instructions, and support. But there are weapons in our arsenal that the enemy and those under his influence cannot detect or fight against. These weapons are so effective that they complete disarm potential battles before they begin.

> The Spirit finds expression in love, joy, peace, endurance, kindness, goodness, faith, gentleness, self-control. Legalism can neither match nor contradict this. There is no law against love. (Galatians 5:22–23)

> Do not be overcome by evil, but overcome evil with good. (Romans 12:21)

Love without any hidden agenda. Utterly detest evil; be glued to good. Take tender care of one another with fondness and affection; esteem one another's value. Do not allow any hesitation to interrupt the rhythm of your zeal; capture the moment; maintain the boiling-point intensity of spirit devotion to the Lord.Delight yourself in the pleasure of expectation; prayer prevails victoriously under pressure. Purpose with resolve to treat strangers as saints; pursue and embrace them with fondness as friends on equal terms of fellowship. Make yourself useful in the most practical way possible.Continue to speak well even if someone wants to take advantage of you; bless and do not blame when you feel exploited. Do not merely act the role in someone else's gladness or grief; feel with them in genuine joy and compassion.Esteem everyone with the same respect; no one is more important than the other. Associate yourself rather with the lowly than with the lofty. Do not distance yourself from others in your own mind.

Two wrongs never make a right. Never retaliate; instead, cultivate the attitude to anticipate only beauty and value in every person you encounter. You have within you what it takes to be everyone's friend, regardless of how they treat you.

Do not bother yourselves to get even, dear ones. Do not let anger or irritation distract you; that which we have in common with one another must set the pace. Scripture confirms that the Lord Himself is the revealer of righteousness.

If your enemy is hungry, feed him; if he is thirsty, give him something to drink. These acts of kindness will certainly rid your enemy of the dross in his mind and win him as a friend.

Do not let evil be an excuse for you to feel defeated,
rather seize the opportunity to turn the situation into
a victory for good. (Romans 12:9–21; Mirror Bible)

Let's bring this home. What is more effective against fear? Is it more fear and intimidation, or genuine love and concern? What will disarm anger, leaving the enemy completely helpless? Kindness, goodness, and gentleness. What will make a hateful person run for the hills? Grace.

Is this kind of warfare easy? I can say with all confidence, absolutely not. Is it powerful? Without a doubt. Why do you think that is? I believe it is because these weapons are not at all familiar to our enemy. He does not know how to fight against them. That is why Calvary was a complete success. How can anyone win a battle when the opponent lays down his life?

There it is again—that grace word. It is everywhere you turn, in one form or another. It is bigger than any intellect or logic; as a matter of fact, it is very illogical from man's point of view. That's what makes it so powerful; it does not originate with man but with God. Grace is a spiritual state, a spiritual position, a spiritual mindset, and a spiritual giant that dwarfs all others. Nothing can defeat God's grace.

I have been visited by hell a few times, and the worst parts of it were the faces that hell used to give me pain. I have known a few people who decided that I was their enemy. (For the life of me I can't figure that one out—I am the nicest person I know!) There were times when I felt like I had a target on my back. What does one do in that situation? Walk in grace.

Ask the Holy Spirit to show you their heart's need. Pray for their healing and restoration. Take the power of God, which abides in you, and walk in the confidence of the cross and in the love that the cross gave to you. That's what you present back to your enemy: Love without condition, respect, and genuine concern for their welfare. Kindness, gentleness, and goodness comes only from heaven. Peace confuses the enemy, and self-control will simply cause them to default.

Is this lifestyle easy? No. Will it hurt? Yes. Then why do it? Why lay down your rights to someone who shows you only evil? That is because grace carries with it Kingdom territory and because graces deposits Kingdom authority wherever you are.

We are living in a new day. We are seeing things from God's view-point, and responding with God's reserves. This is the day described in Romans 8:19–23:

> Our lives now represent the one event every creature anticipated with held breath, standing on tip-toe as it were to witness the unveiling of the sons of God. Can you hear the drum roll? Every creature suffered abuse through Adam's fall; they were discarded like a squeezed-out orange. Creation did not volunteer to fall prey to the effect of the fall. Yet within this stark setting, hope prevails. All creation knows that the glorious liberty of the sons of God sets the stage for their own release from decay.
>
> We sense the universal agony and pain recorded in history until this very moment.
>
> We ourselves feel the grief echo of their groaning within us while we are ready to embrace the original blueprint also of our physical stature to the full consequence of son-ship. What we already now participate in as first fruits of the spirit will blossom into a full gathering of the harvest. (Mirror Bible)

It is exciting, friends!

EVERYDAY EXAMPLES OF TODAY'S HIGH DEFINITION: BEFORE AND AFTER

Food for a laugh, and some for thought.

Do you remember? The days before the words *high definition* were even invented?

Do you remember your first television set? It lived in a lovely wood cabinet, polished to a high shine and housed a twelve- or thirteen-inch screen. With the right timing and turning to the right number on the knob, you would experience the thrill of a lifetime. A picture actually traveled through space and came directly into your living room! Amazing! And—an endless variety, too. There were three channels with choices that all vied for your attention. You could watch Uncle Milty who considered himself the funniest man on earth, then turn to *Masterpiece Theater* for some culture, or a good "shoot-em-up" cowboy story.

There was an occasional glitz, however, called "*snow*" that was aptly named: (the screen resembled a blizzard.) But don't worry, there is another electronic piece of genius called an antenna that is a strange-looking apparatus, placed on top of the television set with connecting wires. When connected correctly, all interference magically vanished—sort of—well, maybe, depending on a few factors. If you turned it slowly, held your breath, stood on one foot with a piece of aluminum foil in one hand—almost—getting close—there! Stop! Don't move—a perfect picture.

Television was a means of entertainment and information about the world around you. It soon became a necessary part of every home. Not only entertaining, it also connected you to the world. You could actually see what was happening in other places. It was a source of seeing what had been unavailable to you before. If you were going to be a well-informed citizen, it was important to see and understand current conditions in your community and beyond. This was a tool, a key to good, calculated decisions in your life. It was a new way of seeing, a new way of understanding.

Let's reminisce a little more. We could watch Ralph threaten to send his wife "To the moon, Alice!" Or if we were in the mood for the thrilling, often scary, but always twisted adventure in *The Twilight Zone*.

I remember tearing through the door after school, going to "the tube" (what is a tube, anyway?), placing myself about twelve inches from the screen, waiting with bated breath for those magical words that sent me to another realm—"Welcome to the Mickey Mouse Club!" Who can forget those adorable kids: Karen, Cubby, the lovely Annette, and Bobby who had a smile so big you had to wonder if he had more teeth than anyone in the world. He would always end the show with the marvelous benediction when we would all sing along with all the reverence you could muster—remember the words?

Okay, let's get serious here. This is only a test. Do you know . . . ?

What was the name of the jeep in the Roy Roger show?

What was the name of the Lone Ranger's horse?

How about the weapon of choice for his Native sidekick, Tonto?

"Out of the blue of the Western sky." Who was that? Do you remember the name of his plane?

What was the name of Buffalo Bill's puppet? They were joined by the clown named _____.

"The many loves of Dobey Gillis," his beatnik friend's name? And the thing he hated to think about?

Do you remember the puppets Beanie and his friend, who happened to be a _____?

Who was Captain Kangaroo's friend?

The talking horse?

Smile! You're on _____.

I'd say that we were adequately entertained. We were also well informed by the reality of local and national news. I was a high school junior in US History class when John Kennedy was assassinated. The images will forever linger in my memory.

The news—wonderful, terrible, thrilling, chilling and exciting—was always, *always* true!

As technology grew, so did our vision and understanding. We are ever expanding our territory. No longer satisfied with images on a screen, we now bring those images into our personal space, surrounding us with new experiences. We are enveloped with 3-D and surround sound right into another reality. We enter this new technology, see what it sees, and feel what it feels.

There are realms that had been hidden. We have gone from spectator to participant. We are awakened to another realm, with another truth.

I am sure you realize that I am no longer referring to this world's technological wonders. All the illustrations cross easily into another realm, the realm of the Spirit. God is bringing His High Definition to new levels, to make His kingdom a reality where we live.

So, as Buzz Lightyear aptly declared: "To infinity—and beyond!"

CHAPTER 10
THE ORIGINAL PLAN

Genesis 1:26 states, "*Then God said, 'Let Us make man in Our image, according to Our likeness.*'" Considering all the gods worshipped around the world today, I would like to know, what God is this?

Now in our world today, we see societies worship demons disguised as gods and where gods are invented by the human mind. We see religions worshipping something or someone: an entity or multitudes of entities.

These gods range in temperament from slightly annoyed to volatile, passive, or vengeful. They must be appeased. Strict obedience is demanded. Sacrifice is required. Sacrifices may include money, penance, service and time given, and devotion shown in a thousand ways. Many are blatantly evil and hateful to anyone who threatens to disagree, even to noncompliants.

These gods have egos. They all claim to possess the truth; some even have a corner on the market. Nearly all of them demand rigid behavior regulations and offer no options.

Pleasing these gods is attainable *only* if you are willing to pay the price, which, in fact, goes up if no effort is made by the worshipper.

Fear is the underlying motivation in the lives of those under the control of these hellish religions. Love is unheard of; it is a completely foreign concept. These gods show no love, no approval and no comfort, joy, or peace.

Outsiders are viewed with pity, suspicion, and even fearful paranoia.

People have sold their soul to these religions in the hope that their eternity will be secure.

There are countless religions in the world today; all clamoring to be heard and obeyed.

All except ONE.

The ONE who was not created by a religious system or dogma.

The ONE who is characterized by creating, not destroying.

The ONE who stands alone in His holiness, His righteousness, and His goodness.

The ONE who is relentlessly kind, always gentle, full of mercy, and abounding in love.

The ONE called Love.

When all the others are taking, this ONE is giving. Not ordinary giving, but He gives in ways far beyond anything man has ever known. Unlike religion that is defined by what it requires, this ONE is defined by what He gives.

He is the ONE who created man and breathed His very life into him. Those who believe this fact find that God's very life spills out of them, thus giving away the exact same life they have received to everyone they encounter.

He is the ONE who gave Himself. If there are sacrifices to be made, He makes them Himself. Why? Because He is love. Catherine of Siena, who lived in the 14th century wrote:

> You, high eternal Trinity, acted as if You were drunk with love, infatuated with your creature . . . You, sweetness itself, stooped to join Yourself with our bitterness. You, Splendor, joined Yourself with darkness; You, Wisdom, with foolishness; You, Life, with death; You, Infinite, with us who are finite.

> What drove You to this?

> Oh priceless love! You showed Your enflamed desire when You ran like a blind man to the cross. A blind man can't see, and neither can a drunken man when he is fast drunk. And thus Christ, almost like someone dead, blind, and drunk, lost Himself for our salvation!

Oh unutterable love. . . . even though You saw all the evils that all your creatures would commit against Your infinite goodness, You acted as if You did not see and set Your eye only on the beauty of Your creature, with whom You fell in love like One drunk and crazy with love. And in love You drew us out of Yourself, giving us being.'

For I know the thoughts that I think toward you, says the Lord, thoughts of peace and not of evil, to give you a future and a hope. (Jeremiah 29:11; NKJV)

Many, O Lord my God, are Your wonderful works which You have done; and Your thoughts toward us cannot be recounted to You in order; if I would declare and speak of them, they are more than can be numbered. (Psalm 40:5 NKJV)

How precious are Your thoughts to me, O God! How great is the sum of them! If I should count them, they would be more in number than the sand. (Psalm 139:17-18 NKJV)

Do you realize that you are being watched over; tenderly, with unfathomable love? Do you realize that you are the constant object of His affection? Abandon yourself to His grace. Lose yourself in His love. Find yourself in His love.

THE ORIGINAL PLAN

God's original plan for mankind is remarkable; it is so far from human logic and reasoning that it takes some people by surprise when they discover it. Others have to think about it for some time before they can make a decision to accept or reject it. There are those who need to figure it all out before they put their faith in it. Good luck with that one!

Man was created in God's very own image and likeness. The word image in Hebrew is *tselem*, meaning resemblance, representative, a

141

model, something to be compared to. Essentially, Adam and Eve were modeled after God. Amazing.

My prayer, as I conclude this book, is that the Holy Spirit will take His truth deep into our hearts, so we will experience what God had in mind for us from before time began. These truths are life changing. They are the truth of the Gospel—the truth that sets people free from every bondage.

SHARE THE JOY

Man was created for pleasure—God's pleasure and ours, too!

So many people cannot put the two words *God* and *pleasure* together in the same thought. I have to wonder why, so I have some questions that need answers. I know that the truth sets me free. Therefore, I believe we are about to experience a divine encounter with the Truth. If I find myself experiencing bondage in some area, I need to know the lie that I am hanging on to.

Truth One: We were created to have an open communication with heaven on a continual basis. We are human beings and spiritual beings at the same time. We are spirit, housed in humanity. Our spirit is eternal, even though the body it is housed in will pass away. That should bring great hope and joy to us, knowing that here on earth we are experiencing just the beginning of eternal life.

Truth Two: We are created to experience heaven and earth simultaneously. Jesus walked on this soil, fully God and fully man, bringing heaven's reality to the earth. Remember His message? The Kingdom of heaven is here. I believe that is precisely what He meant. God made a way for men to live filled with heaven's reality. They fit together, just as planned.

Truth Three: We are created to have productive, interactive encounters with the God of the universe. The word is intimacy. We enjoy long-distance encounters today because of amazing technology. That is not what I am referring to when I speak of our relationship with God. This may sound strange, but our relationship with God is the exact opposite of long-distance. It is as intimate as it can be. Man was physically designed to be a host—a carrier of God. He fits us like a glove. Our mind, our decision-making process, our emotional life, and even our natural bodies yearn for the harmony that comes when the eternal God steps inside of us and wears us like a garment.

Truth Four: We were created to carry out the nature of our Creator, enjoying all of creation and indescribable oneness with God, just like Jesus did when He lived among men. One of the most descriptive scriptures about this relationship is found in John 17. Jesus knew what He was facing, and why He was choosing to do so. The NKJV states:

> Jesus spoke these words, lifted up His eyes to heaven, and said, "Father, the hour has come. Glorify Your Son that Your Son may glorify You. You have given Him authority over all flesh, that he should give eternal life to as many as You have given Him. And this is eternal life, that they may know You, the only true God, and Jesus Christ whom You have sent. I have glorified You on the earth. I have finished the work which You have given me to do. And now, O Father, glorify Me together with Yourself with the glory which I had with You before the world was.
>
> I pray that those who believe in Me all may be one, as You, Father, are in Me, and I in You; that they also may be one in Us. And the glory which You gave me I have given them, that they may be one just as We are one. I in them, and You in Me; that they may be made perfect in one. (excerpts from John 17)

What Jesus was referring to is the very same relationship that He experienced with God, His Father. His desire is for us to know our identity in the same way He understood His identity and that we occupy that reality in the same way He lived it.

This may be new to some readers, but with some research we see that the word *one* in John 17 is the Greek word, *heis,* which translated means, one and the same; or, the same as. How can this be? It is certainly not by human means of any sort, but only by the fulfillment of God's original plan, as we will investigate further.

WHAT DO YOU SEE?

God made a way, not for us to act like Jesus, but to be like Jesus. That is, in the very least, an astounding statement, and one that needs explanation. In order to do that, we need to go back to the very beginning—to God's original plan. Genesis 1:26 states. "*Then God said, 'Let Us make man in Our image, according to Our likeness.'*"

Adam and Eve had it made. Even the place where they lived, Eden, means "pleasure." We need to begin to see that God is pro-pleasure, pro-joy, and pro-delight. I have discovered that God is so much fun to be with. Have you ever been so delighted in His presence that you just couldn't stop laughing or get the giggles at His outrageous love? So many have swallowed the bitter pill that presents God as angry, vengeful, and ready to punish those who get out of line. What if that is a big, fat lie? Let me show you the real One, whose love is so pure it is impossible to fathom and whose motives are always good and full of life.

EDEN

Eden, a place of euphoria, was heaven on earth. Adam and Eve could partake of everything they saw, except one tree. Called the "Tree of the Knowledge of Good and Evil," it was off-limits because it was dangerous to their well-being. The Bible tells us that its fruit looked good, but was deadly when eaten. There was another tree in Eden that they were encouraged to enjoy; the "Tree of Life." This tree had life-giving fruit that gave eternal God-life to the partaker.

We all know what happened. They were not alone in the garden. Disguised in a snake-skin suit, Satan himself delivered his well-planned offer to Eve. It didn't take long for her to take the bait. She was hooked, and offered to share it with Adam. That choice changed mankind forever.

Genesis 3 tells us the story. There are some very interesting facts that are often overlooked. Adam immediately started finding someone to blame. That tells me that there was an instant change in his heart. His finger, of course, pointed directly at Eve, which sounded reasonable since she was the only other human around. However, may I note that Eve got the instructions second-hand? God spoke directly to Adam about the tree; Eve heard it from Adam.

THE ORIGINAL PLAN

Of course, Eve then understood what had happened, and confessed that the serpent had deceived her. This is interesting to me. Eve did not make excuses, but she did discern the truth about the serpent. He was a deceiver. She named it correctly and nailed the serpent. Women are still a particular threat to the darkness; they often carry intuition that is not obvious. Not much has changed since then; men need to figure things out and get to the bottom of an issue. Women tend to feel things out. What is my point? We need each other.

THE LIES

Sadly, Adam and Eve were evicted from their perfect home. Eating the forbidden fruit allowed evil into their pure existence. The serpent's lie we so easily embrace was deceitful. Usually there is a sliver of truth hidden in the lies that deceive. Satan told Eve that God did not want them to be like Him. Not so! God's very heart was to make them in His image and likeness. She was already made in His image. We need to take note of that. Our enemy tells us the very same lie today by distorting the truth of who God says we are in Christ.

Remember the tree was called the knowledge of good and evil. Adam and Even already had experienced God's goodness. It was every-where around them and in them. It was what they lived and breathed. Good things, good relationship, and a good environment was their normal. When someone tries to say that God tried to withhold good-ness from them, it simply is not truth. It was the evil that God was shielding them from.

On that terrible day, God's original plan was handed over to man's enemy, who is bent on his destruction.

I have come to *unlearn* many things about God, things that distort the truth. These things were presented as gospel, when actually they are false assumptions of mankind's beginning, as recorded in the Old Testament of the Bible. I'd like to address these ideas, and perhaps free our minds to see the truth of who God is.

EVICTED!

After sin entered and messed up the ideal experience, after Adam and Eve deliberately disobeyed God and made choices independent of His council, and after their perfect life was marred by sin, the general consensus says that God became angry at them and punished them because of their disobedience and rebellion by being forced out of their home. Mighty angels were even stationed at the entrance of the garden to keep them out. Basically, we are taught that God was mad at them, and that anger carries on today. We hear that message preached today in many ways and in a multitude of places. It sounds something like this: Repent, or you will feel God's wrath!

There have been many times I have sat for an hour of fist-pounding fierceness, declaring that I need to change my behavior so God will accept me. I haven't heard that for some time now, but if I ever encounter another message like that, I am going to remove my miserable, sinning, unworthy carcass from the premises. It is a lie.

PUNISHMENT OR DIVINE MERCY?

When Adam and Eve were literally forced out of Eden, was it harsh punishment from an angry God, or could it be something entirely different that we don't understand? Why is the difference important? Too often we don't look deep enough into the truth of a matter. Let's look at this one.

First, we need to understand that the fruit that grew on the Tree of Life had the power to make eternally permanent the spiritual condition of the person who ate it. That tells me that Adam and Eve had not picked that fruit yet, and that the evil one had to work fast to force their focus on the tree that would destroy them. If they had eaten of the Tree of Life first, it would have secured their righteous relationship with God and nothing could have taken it from them. If they ate the forbidden fruit first, sin would enter their lives, which is precisely what happened. However, if they then ate from the Tree of Life, it would have made their sinful condition eternal. There would be no hope for redemption. They would be eternally lost.

Telling Adam and Eve to leave the Tree of the Knowledge of Good and Evil was not to keep some good from them; it was for their protection. After the fact, it was not anger that caused God to remove them from the garden. It was His mercy. Love is always His motive toward man. Adam and Eve were removed from the tree that would seal their eternal doom.

This is a perfect example of one of the many types of our Redeemer, Jesus Christ, that are found in the Old Testament. Jesus is our Tree of Life. Partaking of that fruit changes us, and we experience His keeping power in our life.

Love, mercy, and grace are always God's motivation toward us. That is His only driving force. To think otherwise is to misjudge Him. Our view of God is crucial to our understanding. It is like looking through colored glasses; it changes everything we see. It colors every part of our life. I want to be sure to get that one right!

Another misconception that surrounds this event in human history is about sin. It is true that after Adam and Eve made the poor choices that they did, sin entered their lives. Nothing would ever be the same again. The deceitful error here is that we are told that God cannot look on sin; therefore, He separated Himself from men.

Is that idea true or false? God cannot look on sin. Have you ever heard these words? Do you know where they are found in the Bible, in reference to God's relationship with man? They aren't. I checked it out. The Bible says nothing about God's inability to look on sin. However, religion has made a doctrine of that statement.

I have even heard it spoken from a pulpit recently. The belief is that God cannot look on sin; therefore, we need to repent and accept Jesus to avoid hell. If that sounds familiar to anyone, I have good news! That is not how God operates in our lives. It is gross error because it goes to the heart of our identity and changes it into a dangerous lie. Why is this teaching dangerous? It carries the idea that God separated Himself from man. He is somewhere "out there," far away from us and our concerns. People are taught today that God is still filled with wrath against man's rebellion, and as sinners He cannot even look our way.

This is not true of God. Let's take a good look at it. God did not remove Himself from mankind. He came near to us and entered our world with the express purpose to redeem us back to Himself. Any teaching that tells you about a distant God simply does not know the truth of who He is.

What is so dangerous about this line of thinking and believing? It doesn't stop with the error that God is distant and aloof and cares only about sin in people's lives. It goes on to give the indication that Calvary was all about God's anger against man. This teaching says that Jesus stepped in, took the punishment, thus paying God off for our sin.

There is a term for this: penal substitution. The idea that Jesus died to "pay off" an angry Father. The truth is, Jesus was not crucified to purchase the Father's love for us or to change God's mind about sinful man. Jesus was not changing God; He was changing me! Jesus took my sin to the cross. When He died, my sinful nature died. It was buried with Him in the grave, and it stayed in the grave. When Jesus rose from death, I was resurrected with Him, with a new nature that is called God's righteousness. Jesus did this one time only for all humanity (past, present, and future). Once, for all. Those words are found throughout Paul's teaching.

I have also recently heard someone say that when Jesus cried out in anguish, "My God, My God, why have your forsaken Me?" during His last agonizing moment of life, it was again because God could not look on sin, and therefore on Jesus, who at that moment was carrying the sin of the world. Thus the conclusion that He felt forsaken by His Father. This says that God turned away. He left Jesus, His beloved Son, forsaken, alone, and broken during His most horrifying hours. What kind of father would do such a thing? This is another dangerous teaching.

It misrepresents God, misrepresents Jesus' atonement, and misrepresents the cross. It lays a totally false foundation of our faith. It is a fear-based theology that focuses on guilt and condemnation. It is not truth.

With this type of teaching being spoken from pulpits today, it is no wonder why many people who believe in God aren't found in church on Sunday. It is no wonder why my entire life was consumed with making God happy! It left me with a false understanding of who God really is.

Was God's wrath poured out on Jesus as He hung on that cross? Yes! It was His wrath against sin. God was angry, all right—angry at what sin had done to those He created and loved.

The cross was not about paying God off. It was about *removing the very thing that separated man from Him.* It was all about reconciling us back to God. It was about fulfilling absolutely every requirement of the law, and instituting a new law based on the Spirit of life in Christ Jesus. You will find that in Romans 8:1–3.

The cross was about man's healing, our restoration, our redemption, our sanctification, and our freedom. The cross was about us. It was not about averting wrath; it was about removing the cause of our alienation. It was not about God's punishment; it was about His redemptive love.

Why, then did Jesus cry out about being forsaken? I believe He was quoting a very well-known scripture in Psalm 22 that people standing there would completely recognize and understand. This song of David begins with those very words. It was read and known by the religious leaders of Jesus' day. It is a prophetic message about the coming Messiah. It was, to them, like the Lord's Prayer or the 23rd Psalm are to us today. If I were to speak the first works of either of those scriptures, you would, out of memory, continue with the next line: "Our Father, which art in heaven" . . . "hallowed be Thy Name." It is my belief that when Jesus uttered those words, the hearers went immediately in their memories to the psalm that referred to the Messiah. I think Jesus was saying, "This is that, people. You are seeing with your very eyes the fulfillment of that prophecy. I am the One David was speaking about; right now, this very moment, that prophecy is being fulfilled."

The Father never once turned away from Jesus. He never turns away from you or me. No matter what the situation looks like or feels like, we know that God is holding us close and that He will never let go.

STICK TO THE ORIGINAL PLAN

Even amidst all the sin and sin's effect on the earth, even though sin separated men from God, even though men turned to love other things and other gods, even when we loved sin more than Him, God still sticks to His original plan—"Let Us make man in Our own image." That plan is all about union, oneness, intimacy, and relationship. If you hear any teaching that separates us, throw it away.

God is about bringing us into His domain, including us and making us part of His life. He supplies all we need to become part of His existence. I believe religion had turned God's original plan into something He did not intend.

There are those today who have great reasoning abilities. Their skills in the art of logical deductions are unsurpassed. They can maneuver their way around mysteries and come up with sensible, reasonable conclusions. It works well in society, in the workplace, and even in relationships. When it comes to God's ways, however, it is absolutely useless. In that arena, we can think ourselves right into a bottomless pit.

God's ways are so far above ours that to even try to reach them is exercise in futility. Simply put, man cannot figure God out. I believe it is because at the root of all God is and all He does is a love so beyond comprehension that it doesn't fit in any box man can create.

So it is with God's original plan. There have been so many attempts at putting it into a box called "logic" that have caused more confusion and questions than answers.

Another endeavor at cracking this puzzle is the belief that after the fall of man messed everything up, God had to come up with a Plan B: some way to fix the situation. This reasoning says that God would visit earth from time to time, drop in on someone He had his eye on for a special assignment.

ABRAM

I can imagine God's conversation with Abram—"Hey there, Abram! How's your day going? I have a message for you. Brace yourself, this will be a stretch for your faith. . . . I have chosen you to be the father of many nations. You will have so many descendants that they will be countless, as the sands of the sea." God's number one choice to father a nation was a ninety-plus-year-old man whose wife, nearly the same age, has never had children. Perfect! You are the one!

God sees what we are blind to. Take a good look in the mirror and then ask this question: what do I see? Follow that question with another one: what does God see? God sees far beyond what we see, past the past, past the present, and into the future. Into potential only He can create.

MOSES

From birth, God had big plans for Moses. Through a series of adventures Moses is finally ready to hear about God's purposes. His response to God's message? Moses goes from disbelief to interrogation to whining to excuses and then starts over, trying to wiggle out of this mission.

We know that he eventually found himself leading millions of family members on a forty-year journey to the place God had promised them centuries before. While camping around Mount Sinai, God called Moses up to the mountain to speak to Him face-to-face and give instructions on how to live the right way.

This is also known as God's Plan B. The sin problem was fixed. Now we know what God wants from us. He gave us a hand-written list of laws to live by. When followed and obeyed, we might just fulfil God's original plan for mankind.

The case was solved; the original plan problem was fixed. It sounds good and looks reasonable—or not. If we look a little closer, we discover some interesting things about how God related to those people He called His own. During the years before the law was given, God provided absolutely everything they needed for their journey. He gave them food, water, and even the shoes on their feet that did not wear out during that time. Their health was good, too. That's where God's heart for people is; *to do it all for us—to be our complete source for everything we may need in life.* The Ten Commandments were given after the people turned down God's offer to continue being their source. Man would rather work for what he wants than be the recipient of such amazing grace. So, God let them have their way and gave them lists of requirements for a happy life.

Herein lies another false assumption about God's plan, which is still being taught today. The Mosaic Law given to Moses on Mount Sinai, written by God's own hand must be the answer to God's original plan. Even that amazing, hand-written document, which was given by God Himself, was not His original plan. There was no Plan B.

Many people, even today, believe completely in a false doctrine. It has been adopted and embraced by Christians worldwide. Simply put, they believe that by adhering to and obeying those commandments people will be on God's list of righteous ones. They believe, because of their good choices and because they are in agreement with the law and behave accordingly, God will smile on them, and they will go to heaven someday. That is their destiny for one reason only—they earned it.

ENTER: GOD WITH SKIN ON

Even after the New Covenant was established by God's Son, Jesus Christ; even after Calvary, people believe that the Law plus Jesus secures their eternity. Do they believe in Jesus' atoning work on the cross? Yes, but often for the wrong reasons. They believe that Jesus died for their sin, and they accept that into their lives and then proceed to live as though they still need to hold tightly to the Law, plus any New Testament commandments they can find. The better I am at keeping all this up, the more favor I have with the Lord. The result is a life filled with commandments and laws that God expects us to perform; if we do well enough, we may fulfill His original plan.

Again, this logic appeals to man's reasoning and ego. It scratches that itch to do everything in my power to be the best I can be. It appeals to my pride.

Men have been wrestling with this from the beginning. Let's take a look at what we have covered so far:

Original plan: God said, "Let Us make man in Our own image."

Sin: spoiled everything.

Plan B: the law.

Close, but no cigar. Why? What happened? Why is this not a good plan? Putting it simply, the law and grace do not mix. They cannot co-exist.

What was the purpose of the Law? First, it was to show God's perfect standard, and second, it was to reveal what sin is. People need to have something they must do: a set of rules, special prayers, penance, and so on. This sounds reasonable from our point of view. We sometimes forget that God's ways are so far above our thinking that we miss it completely. So, what do we do with the law? How can we be made in God's image?

THE ANSWER

Jesus was the fulfillment of God's original plan. At Calvary God made the Mosaic Law obsolete. End of discussion. The law was wonderful until it was no longer necessary. Colossians 2:14 (NKJV) states: "Jesus, having wiped out the handwriting of requirements that was against us, which was contrary to us. And He has taken it out of the way, having nailed it to the cross."

Why was the Law no longer necessary? Every single requirement was met by God Himself, Jesus Christ, on the cross at Calvary. That was the fulfillment of God's original plan. Adam and Eve were made in God's image. Do you remember what the serpent told Eve? Part of it said that man would be just like God, inferring that was not true at that time. Wait a minute. She already was like God, made in His image and likeness.

I love it when the Holy Spirit highlights a word and gives us understanding about it. Usually it is a tiny word that is often easily overlooked. This time it is the word *Us*. God said, "let Us make man in Our own image." I don't see my name anywhere in this process. Do you suppose that is the point?

What if this entire subject was God's project? What if He wants to do it all? What if my involvement actually acts as interference, and serves only to stop my progress?

MAN'S LOGIC SAYS:

So far we have looked at man's interpretation of the whole process entitled God's design for mankind. I want to take a careful look at what man has deduced:

Original plan: Let Us make man in Our own image.

Enter: sin marred the God image, distanced God from mankind.

Plan B: the Mosaic Law—commandments to make us holy, thus putting us back under God's plan.

Calvary: Jesus came to appease God's anger at mankind for sinning in the first place. Now God can come close again when we walk worthy of the Lord; when certain conditions are met.

Conclusion (man's reasoning): Our spirit is redeemed, but our soul and body require our constant and diligent maintenance, which, by the way, we will be obsessed with every day of our lives. Does this sound familiar? Making lifelong adjustments? Are we sanctified by degrees, or by levels on the perfect-o-meter?

Where is the gospel message in this line of thinking? It isn't. But this exact message has been preached for centuries as truth. What is wrong with it? Why would I call this seemingly wonderful plan, which is backed by some scripture, a false doctrine?

May I explain? The difference is huge. The issue is an under-emphasis on Jesus' finished work, and an over-emphasis on my role in reaching the goal. Jesus did it all. The incarnation changed everything. We simply need to wake up to that fact.

DOCTRINE OF DEMONS

This doctrine dates back to New Testament times. A heresy was creeping into the early church. John called it the spirit of antichrist. It is called Gnosticism, later called Dualism. The separation between God and man is at its roots. The first thing this doctrine teaches is that because of sin, God separated Himself from man. We know that is not the truth. But it goes further than that; it taught that the spirit is holy, but every other part of man is unholy and needs to be sanctified—a process that takes the rest of your life. Therefore it concludes that anything connected to the soul realm or the body is evil.

During John's time they were teaching that Jesus did not have a human body (because the body is evil). They taught that Jesus was a spirit that revealed itself to man. That's why John said, in his first letter, chapter 4, that anyone who does not believe that Jesus came in the flesh was of the antichrist. Today that same teaching is called "Christ-consciousness."

Let's look down through the centuries. Originating from Gnosticism, it was also taught by Aristotle and then Plato put another spin on it. It is from Greek thought, not Hebrew. You may recognize some of it still being taught today. These are some of what you will hear:

- You still have a sin nature. (Dirty soul/clean spirit.) This reminds me of the cartoons shown years ago of "shoulder angels," each one trying to persuade the person to follow their advice. It has also been illustrated as having a good dog/bad dog syndrome inside your soul, both fighting for control.
- Since the body and soul are evil, you have a lifelong burden to crucify your flesh. This means that you must chip off everything that is not perfect in your opinion and in the opinion of others. It is often referred to as pruning off dead, unproductive branches, also known as the sin nature. God isn't interested in pruning the old nature. He pulled the whole rotten thing out of the ground, destroying it completely, and then planted a new seed called God's righteousness.
- Emotions are evil. Keep them under the rug.
- Take heart, however! When you die and go to heaven, you will be perfect. (What? Death makes me holy?)
- Christians aren't perfect, just forgiven. Read the book, please.
- While you are on the earth, separate yourself from the world. Keep yourself away from physical, material, and emotional contaminants,
- Reject all comforts.
- Root out all evil.

Do these things sound noble, even righteous? What is wrong with this line of thinking? Why did 1 John 4:16 call it the spirit of antichrist? Those are extremely harsh words, not to be taken lightly. We need to pay attention.

The first argument is taken from 1 Thessalonians 5:23–24.

May God Himself, the God of peace, sanctify you through and through. May your whole spirit, soul and body be kept blameless at the coming of our Lord Jesus Christ. The One who calls you is faithful and He will do it. (NKJV)

The idea here is that mankind is made of three parts. It also comes not from Hebrew thought, but from Greek. Both the Old and New Testament use the words *spirit* and *soul* interchangeably. Hebrew thought says that man is made of two parts: visible and invisible. The verse in 1 Thessalonians is the only place in the Bible that states a three-part person. However, we can see how easily it fits into dualism theology. The apostles had no teaching about this at all.

The word *may* in this scripture is not in the original Greek manuscript. (It makes it sound like something that hasn't happened yet.) This verse does not indicate that sanctification is a process. Paul is talking about God preserving you—all of you, rolled up into His holiness. Perfection is not coming; it has already been given. You cannot preserve something you don't already have. The kicker is that Paul tells us that it is God who guards us until the end. We need to stay out of His business.

My redemption, sanctification, righteousness, holiness—all of it, was finished at Calvary. I had absolutely nothing to do with it at all. To that I say, with great gratitude, thank You, Jesus.

I don't know how many parts of me there are. It doesn't matter because the blood of the cross has covered them all. God has every single cell in His care and has promised me that they will stay in His care forever. Men have made a doctrine out of this verse, along with others, and created something that was not intended by the author—that the atoning work of Jesus was not complete, and there are parts of us that are our responsibility to fix.

There is another scripture that is often quoted when discussing man's sanctification. It is found in Hebrews 4:12, where Paul is speaking of God's Word being able to divide soul and spirit, joints and marrow: "For the Word of God is living and powerful, and sharper than any two-edged sword, piercing even to the division of soul and spirit, and of joints and marrow" (NKJV).

Notice the word *piercing* used here. It is the same in every translation: "piercing," not slicing. What is Paul speaking of here? He is encouraging people to leave behind all struggle to obtain salvation or overcome the sin nature. Verse 11 urges us to enter into the rest provided by God, wherein He has done everything needed to secure our redemption and sanctification. God's Word is able to pierce into the depth of our being, directly into the heart of the matter. This is about discernment. It has nothing to do with how many parts we are made of, nor is it about the need for separation. God covers it all.

The spirit of the antichrist is any theology that replaces what Jesus has done with what we must do to attain any spiritual level or place. We have been at war with ourselves for centuries. I have wonderful news! The war is over!

God is not about separation. He is about union. He is about incarnation. John 1:14 gives us a wonderful picture of what this means:

> And the Word became flesh and dwelt among us, and we beheld His glory, the glory as of the only begotten of the Father, full of grace and truth. (NKJV)

> Suddenly the invisible eternal Word takes on visible form! The Incarnation! In Him, and now confirmed in us! The most accurate tangible display of God's eternal thought finds expression in human life! The Word became a human being; we are His address; He resides in us! He captivates our gaze! The glory we see there is not a religious replica; He is the authentic begotten Son. The glory (that Adam lost) returns in fullness! Only grace can communicate truth in such complete context! (Mirror)

God's desire to become one with the human race is most clearly revealed in Jesus Christ. God's original plan is fulfilled in Him. Am I saying that we don't have a choice about this? Absolutely, without exception, yes! That is exactly what I am saying. God's original plan for us, and the fulfillment of that plan through the person on His Son, Jesus Christ, was entirely His doing. Not only did Jesus finish well, we cannot reverse or undo any of it. It is finished, completed completely. No strings attached, no conditions whatsoever, and no additions, either. You can, however, say no. Hebrews describes the children of Israel who did not enter their God-given promise by choosing not to believe.

IMAGE BEARERS

Colossians 2:9-10 states: "For in Him dwells all the fullness of the Godhead bodily; and you are complete in Him, who is the head of all principality and power." There is God's original plan for mankind, fulfilled by Jesus, for us.

Jesus is our redemption, our salvation, our sanctification, and our holiness. It is His holiness we carry. God's original plan is forever finished in Christ. We cannot choose to make ourselves anything at all. That choice was made for us and fulfilled for us. Our part is to simply recognize what God has already finished.

You are in a very present, active, living union with God because of the incarnation: the life, death and resurrection of Jesus Christ. Second Corinthians 5:21 tells us that God provided much more than our redemption. He made Him who knew no sin to become sin for us, that we might be the righteousness of God in Christ. That is our identity. That is the ultimate fulfillment of God's original plan.

BUT WAIT! THERE'S MORE!

Are we then finished when we connect with God? Is there a process involved? The answer is yes for both questions. When we are in Christ, we are complete just as Jesus is complete. And yes, there is a process that occurs, purely because we are learning the details of Jesus' redemptive act. The process is the discovery of what Jesus has already accomplished and what God has already deposited in us. It is not a process of searching out imperfections and killing them off. It is a process of encountering the truth of our total sanctification.

When the Holy Spirit puts His finger on something new I need to know, He is literally pointing to my next miracle. He is showing me what is already mine in Christ, and how to appropriate that into my life. As layers of truth are revealed to us, we are changed by His Spirit.

> Where the Spirit of the Lord is, there is liberty. And
> we all, with unveiled face, beholding as in a mirror the
> glory of the Lord are being transformed into the same
> image from glory to glory, just as by the Spirit of the
> Lord. (2 Corinthians 3:17–18)

You are evidence that God's original plan is right here, right now. By God's own power, that plan has been restored in you. The days of struggling to find some new place of achievement are over. No longer working for God's righteousness and holiness, you now rest in them.

God's original plan, fulfilled by Jesus Christ, is living in us!

Every day becomes a new adventure; every minute, every second, every moment filled with the reality of being full of the essence of God's nature. What part of our human experience is "secular," without Jesus, devoid of the life of the Father, Son and Spirit? Parenthood? Work? Play? Gardening, golf, teaching, shopping, baseball, school?

God has woven the "ordinary" business of our natural lives into the fabric of His existence. It is not only you walking around, doing ordinary things, it is Christ in you filling the ordinary with God's kingdom reality. Just as Jesus lived, we live. In Him we live and move and have our being. In us He lives and moves and has His being and expression.

God holds all things together, and all things are sustained in Him. He truly exists in all and through all.

The natural and spiritual life were never intended to be separated from one another. That is fear-based religious propaganda. When God finished creating, He looked around—and called it good. Before the foundation of the world, God knew you. You were the object of His love.

ONE MORE STORY

Come with me in your imagination way, way back, long before time meant anything. God was thinking about His creation. The Father looks forward in time and stops for a moment. The Son and Holy Spirit are watching intently. "I see a girl . . ." the Father speaks, "brown curly hair, black eyes. A little small for her age, but it doesn't matter to her. She is a thousand times bigger on the inside! She will understand My love in a great way. She will know My heart for her."

Jesus breaks in the conversation. "Yes! I see her, too! She is going to know Me intimately. That will be her passion in life . . . to know Me in the fullest way possible. She will know Me in truth. She will pursue Me, and I will run to her. Together we will dance through life." After a short pause, Jesus breaks into delightful laughter. "I am going to give her a great imagination. She will be able to visualize a project and have the ability to see it come to life. It will give us both great joy. Joy! Yes! Laughter will never be far from her lips, and always in her heart."

The Holy Spirit, trying to get a word in, says with great excitement, "I see her, too! Oh, this is going to be fun! I will be as close as her heart-beat. We will be in constant communication, her mind being filled with the truth she longs for. Hey! We will even have a special song that belongs to us alone! Oh! I am so excited!"

The three talked and laughed at the future they see, giving each other high fives and then looked at one another. They were reading each other's thoughts and expressions. Okay. Are you ready? There was a moment's pause in anticipation. "LET THERE BE LIGHT!"

CHAPTER 11

IMAGINE THAT!

Therefore I also, after I heard of your faith in the Lord Jesus and your love for all the saints, do not cease to give thanks for you, making mention of you in my prayers: that the God of our Lord Jesus Christ, the Father of glory, may give you the spirit of wisdom and revelation in the knowledge of Him, the eyes of your understanding being enlightened, that you may know what is the hope of His calling, what are the riches of the glory of His inheritance in the saints. (Ephesians 1:15–17)

Eye has not seen, nor ear heard, nor have entered into the heart of man the things which God has prepared for those who love Him. But God has revealed them to us through His Spirit. For the Spirit searches all things, yes, the deep things of God. For what man knows the things of a man except the spirit of the man which is in him? Even so no one knows the things of God except the Spirit of God. Now we have received, not the spirit of the world, but the Spirit who is from God, that we might know the things that have been freely given to us by God. (1 Corinthians 2:9–12)

I have learned so much during this amazing journey. One thing I will always anticipate learning about is the never-ending glory when God reveals His imagination to me. If God's imagination is a new thought, look around. Everywhere I look I see the Creator's imagination in the glory of His creation. If that is true, why question the imagination He has given men?

I have given the Holy Spirit absolute freedom and permission to remind me of this whenever my heart is affected by life's situations and my mind wants to follow suit.

The first scripture I quoted carries a most important secret. When this was revealed to me, it opened a universe of new thought and creativity. This verse says that the eyes of our understanding are enlightened. The wonderful meaning of the word *understanding* here is imagination.

Religion has forever tried to tell me that imagination is an evil thing and should be avoided. For years I fought with myself over my oversized imagination. I don't anymore. I believe it is His Spirit in me that gives me a creative bent. The closer I get to the Creator, the more His creativity is seen through me.

People may argue that man's imagination can produce dark things. That is true if that man isn't connected to God. Ephesians 4:18–20, 21–22 gives us insight into this subject:

> This I say, therefore, and testify in the Lord, that you should no longer walk as the rest of the Gentiles walk, in the futility of their mind, having their understanding darkened, being alienated from the life of God, because of the ignorance that is in them, because of the blindness of their heart; Who, being past feeling, have given themselves over to lewdness, to work all uncleanness with greediness. But you have not so learned Christ . . . and be renewed in the spirit of your mind, and put on the new man according to God, in true righteousness and holiness.

How can one tell the difference? Check it by the fruit of the Spirit in Galatians 5. That describes God's fruit, produced in and through those who submit to Him. There are many amazingly creative people in the world today. God has placed that gift in them. Some acknowledge that fact, and some do not. When creativity creates in the spectator the awareness of love, joy, peace, longsuffering, kindness, goodness, faithfulness, gentleness, and self-control, I know the source is God.

What if, when sourced in God, my imagination is actually what God sees for my life? Dare I entertain such a thought? I think so! If I believe what He says, my imagination suggests only a fraction of what God wants for me.

I have come from being works-driven to Presence-motivated; from thinking God only visits those who meet His approval to being a habitation where His Spirit lives and moves and has His being. I have come from trying to live for Jesus to letting Him live His life through me. I have come from the bondage of my own making to the freedom secured for me by Jesus Christ on Calvary.

I understand the struggle so many Christians suffer. I am learning things God wishes Christians knew about Christianity. I desire above all to share those things with anyone willing to listen. That is my passion; that is what drives me.

I have come a long way, and yet I have only just begun.

CPSIA information can be obtained
at www.ICGtesting.com
Printed in the USA
FFOW03n2004030118
44344864-44008FF